W9-CDJ-854

ESSENTIALS

OF

FAMILY THERAPY

A THERAPIST'S GUIDE TO EIGHT APPROACHES

WILLIAM M. WALSH
JAMES A. McGRAW
University of Northern Colorado

ESSENTIALS
OF

FAMILY THERAPY
A THERAPIST'S GUIDE TO EIGHT APPROACHES

WILLIAM M. WALSH
JAMES A. MCGRAW
University of Northern Colorado

LOVE PUBLISHING COMPANY®
Denver • London • Sydney

Library of Congress Catalog Card Number 95-75401

Copyright © 1996 Love Publishing Company
Printed in the U.S.A.
ISBN 0-89108-239-5

CONTENTS

PREFACE

The purpose of this book is to provide an overview of a number of popular approaches to family therapy and to point out the similarities and differences in the various approaches. Chapter 1 provides a brief overview of family therapy models in general and discusses the underlying tenets of systems theory as it applies to family therapy models. To varying degrees, each of the family therapy models described here is based on a systemic paradigm.

In each of the next eight chapters, a particular family therapy model is addressed. Chapter 2 describes communication/ validation family therapy. Chapter 3 discusses Bowenian theory. Chapter 4 looks at structural family therapy. Chapter 5 addresses strategic family therapy. Chapter 6 examines the Milan systemic family therapy model. Chapter 7 describes solution-focused brief family therapy. And Chapter 8 examines Adlerian family therapy. Chapter 9 looks at integrative family therapy, and the final chapter briefly describes seven additional approaches to family therapy.

In each of the eight chapters addressing a particular family therapy model, the chapter begins with some background information and then moves on to historical influences, philosophy, theoretical tenets, functional and dysfunctional effects on families, assessment and diagnosis, goals of treatment, the treatment process, techniques, the role of the therapist, and an evaluation of the model's effectiveness. These chapters are not exhaustive reviews of the respective family therapy models but rather are brief condensations of the essential components of these models. For further inquiry, readers are encouraged to review the primary sources indicated at the beginning of each chapter as well as the references listed at the end of each chapter.

ACKNOWLEDGMENTS

We wish to thank Susan Jackson and Kathy Kravits for their invaluable assistance in the preparation of the manuscript.

A Brief Overview of Family Therapy Models

The theories of family therapy outlined in this book differ from one another on numerous characteristics, yet they all can be classified as interpersonal or family systems models. These interpersonal or systemic models of personality and counseling are differentiated from intrapsychic or individual models, the other major paradigm in the helping professions. Intrapsychic models are predicated on different philosophical assumptions and entail divergent ways of conceptualizing and working with human concerns. Many individuals in the helping professions were initially trained in intrapsychic models of psychology; consequently, the mental shift to a systemic paradigm can be difficult and confusing. For example, a clinician may assume he or she is using an interpersonal approach because several family members are present in the session. In actuality, the clinician may be using an intrapsychic model with the family. Conversely, the interpersonal or family systems approach may be used even when only one individual is present in the session.

This introductory chapter provides an overview of intrapsychic and interpersonal models, describing the historical origins and philosophical foundations of each model. It is important to remember that there are some overlapping areas between intrapsychic and interpersonal models and that some differences are subject to interpretation. The intent of this chapter is twofold: to enable the reader to have a clearer and more accurate understanding of the foundations of intrapsychic and interpersonal systemic models of therapy, and to provide a basic overview of systemic thinking, upon which the interpersonal family therapy models in this book are based.

THE INTRAPSYCHIC PARADIGM

The intrapsychic or individual paradigm has a long history in the formative years of the discipline of psychology. Theories of human behavior arise out of the cultural and temporal context in which they are embedded, and the advent of modern psychology dates back to the late nineteenth century. Some of the early pioneers in the development of psychotherapy include Sigmund Freud, B. F. Skinner, and Carl Rogers. The thinking of these early pioneers in psychotherapy was grounded in a Western, positivistic belief system. This belief system reflected the philosophical tenets of individuals such as Sir Isaac Newton, René Descartes, and Francis Bacon.

Within a Newtonian/Cartesian worldview, human behavior is understood to be based on the following four assumptions. First, the laws of nature and human psychological processes are subject to the same laws as are physical bodies. Second, human behavior and psychological processes can be studied through the scientific method, which entails objective observation, reductionism, and experimental control. Third, mechanistic cause and effect relationships can explain reality and human behavior. And finally, reality can be perceived and measured objectively. Capra (1983) suggests that the psychoanalytic view of human behavior was closely related to these assumptions of Newtonian mechanics.

A metaphor that has been used to describe this paradigm is "humans as machines." Intrapsychic models of personality and counseling adhered to these characteristics of the physical sciences to varying degrees. Some theorists felt that psychology could be a science only by modeling itself rigorously after the physical sciences (e.g., Watson's view of behaviorism). Other theorists acknowledged that human behavior may be less subject to deterministic laws and that humans could be more self-directed (e.g., Rogers' person-centered approach).

Early models of psychology viewed individuals and their internal processes as the seat of pathology and as the object of therapeutic intervention. Modern theories of personality and counseling have extended and revised the initial formulations upon which these models were based while preserving most of the fundamental intrapsychic presuppositions. Numerous authors detail the historical and philosophical basis of the intrapsychic paradigm of psychology. A particularly useful book to review for an in-depth inquiry is *Human Change Processes* (Mahoney, 1991).

THE INTERPERSONAL PARADIGM

Throughout history individuals have espoused ideas similar to systemic thinking. A systemic worldview has a long tradition in various belief systems and is frequently found in religion, particularly in Taoism and Buddhism. Von Bertalanffy (1968) cites Aristotle's holistic and teleological worldview, Leibniz's hierarchy of monads, and the dialectical structure of thought espoused by Hegel and Marx as historical predecessors of general systems theory. More recently, some of the revolutionary concepts in modern physics (e.g., relativity, the uncertainty principle, and quantum mechanics) have reinforced a paradigm shift to a more systemic orientation.

Interpersonal models are based on different philosophical assumptions than are intrapsychic models. These interpersonal models all focus on the importance of the family system in understanding an individual's behavior. Because of this orientation, a working understanding of systems theory is essential to fully appreciate the potential value of these models. Gurman and Kniskern (1986) include the following characteristics as core concepts of general systems theory: organization, control, energy, and time and space. Let's take a closer look at these characteristics.

Components of a system relate to each other in some consistent fashion, and the system is structured by those relationships (Goldenberg & Goldenberg, 1991). Some of the characteristics that define an organization include wholeness, boundaries, and a hierarchy. Wholeness simply means that the organization is greater than the sum of its parts. All organizations have limits. These boundaries define a border that separates the family system from other elements of the environment, making the family a distinct entity. Inside the family, the boundaries define separations between the subsystems of the family (Schilson, 1991). The vertical structure within a family system is the hierarchy of the system. This structure usually relates to the degree of influence one member has over another member.

Systems tend to be self-regulating; that is, systems tend to exist in a relatively steady state for substantial periods of time. This is referred to as homeostasis, a dynamic equilibrium in which the system functions without undue stress on its component parts (Umbarger, 1983). Feedback provides the impetus for change within a system. Feedback, the return of a portion of the output of a system back into the system, serves a regulatory function (Nichols & Schwartz, 1991). Control in a system arises through feedback.

The quantity and direction of energy in a system have an impact on the organization and functioning of that system. Entropy, the tendency of a system to go into disorder, brings disorganization, and an undifferentiated form may result (Bateson, 1972). Negentropy describes the tendency of an open system to be flexible and open to new experience and to change or discard interaction patterns that are no longer usable (Kantor & Lehr, 1975). Both of these energy sources act on systems.

Systems exist within a context of material reality and time. As previously noted, theories of human behavior are a function of the cultural and temporal zeitgeist. The evolution of family systems thinking exemplifies this position in that systemic thinking is compatible with modern developments in physics (e.g., nonexistence of objective/detached observation, refutation of linear cause and effect) rather than the Newtonian model of physics.

General systems theory was adapted to the conceptualization of human behavior in social systems by the pioneers of family therapy. Common tenets of family systems models of therapy include the following:

❖ The whole is greater than the sum of its constituent parts (a concept initially credited to Aristotle that later became fundamental to Gestalt psychology).

❖ Components of a system can be understood only within the context of the whole system. Since human behavior arises within a social system, it can be understood only within this context.

❖ Attributions of linear cause and effect are replaced by notions of circular, simultaneous, and reciprocal cause and effect.

❖ A change in one part of a social system (e.g., an individual family member) affects all other parts of that system (e.g., the entire family).

❖ The tendency in a system is to seek homeostasis or equilibrium. This balance-seeking function serves to maintain stability and sometimes prevents change.

❖ When a family is out of equilibrium, feedback mechanisms attempt to bring the family back into balance.

❖ The methods used to restore equilibrium (e.g., identified patients, attempted solutions to problems) can become problems themselves.

❖ Interventions from an interpersonal/family systems perspective focus on relationships within the entire family system rather than on one individual in the family (i.e., the identified patient).

Seminal thinkers in the development of family systems theory such as Gregory Bateson, Murray Bowen, Salvador Minuchin, and Jay Haley have added their own formulations to this mode of thinking; therefore they differ on some specifics of family functioning and clinical practice. Theorists and practitioners who fall into the interpersonal or systemic classification also differ on the degree to which they hold to a systemic paradigm. For example, Haley is typically seen as a systems purist while Virginia Satir's model combines elements of an intrapsychic perspective within a systemic paradigm. And more recent theorists such as Walsh (1980) have developed integrative models of family therapy that combine intrapsychic and systemic components into a theoretically coherent and consistent structure.

SOME CAVEATS TO REMEMBER

Ludwig von Bertalanffy, the founder of general systems theory, juxtaposed the intrapsychic (mechanistic) and the interpersonal models in this way:

> The mechanistic world view, taking the play of physical particles as ultimate reality, found its expression in a civilization which [glorified] physical technology that has led eventually to the catastrophes of our time. Possibly the model of the world as a great organization can help to reinforce the sense of reverence for the living which we have almost lost in the last sanguinary decades of human history. (von Bertalanffy, 1968, p. 49)

It is useful to remember that there is no "purely correct" worldview. Both intrapsychic and interpersonal models are based on assumptions; therefore it is not accurate to say that either paradigm is right or wrong. Both intrapsychic and interpersonal models are useful, given the appropriate context, and both paradigms have contributed to our understanding of and ability to intervene in human behavior. It is crucial that therapists remain cognizant of the model from which they operate (including its assumptions, applications, and limitations) so that their conceptualizations and interventions remain theoretically consistent.

REFERENCES

Bateson, G. (1972). *Steps to an ecology of mind.* New York: Chandler.

Capra, F. (1983). *The turning point: Science, society, and the rising culture.* Toronto: Bantam Books.

Goldenberg, I., & Goldenberg, H. (1991). *Family therapy: An overview.* Pacific Grove, CA: Brooks/Cole.

Gurman, A., & Kniskern, D. (Eds.). (1986). *Handbook of family therapy.* New York: Brunner/Mazel.

Kantor, D., & Lehr, W. (1975). *Inside the family.* San Francisco: Jossey-Bass.

Mahoney, M. (1991). *Human change processes: The scientific foundations of psychotherapy.* New York: Basic Books.

Nichols, M., & Schwartz, R. (1991). *Family therapy: Concepts and methods* (2nd ed.). Boston: Allyn and Bacon.

Schilson, E. (1991). Strategic therapy. In A. M. Horne & J. L. Passmore (Eds.), *Family counseling and therapy.* Itasca, NY: F. E. Peacock.

Umbarger, C. (1983). *Structural family therapy.* New York: Grune & Stratton.

von Bertalanffy, L. (1968). *General systems theory.* New York: Braziller.

Walsh, W. (1980). *A primer in family therapy.* Springfield, IL: Charles C. Thomas.

Communication/ Validation Family Therapy

法律上有效如.

❖ **MAJOR THEORIST: Virginia Satir** ❖

PRIMARY SOURCES FOR FURTHER READING

Peoplemaking, Satir (1972)
Helping Families to Change, Satir, Stachowiak, & Taschman (1975)
Making Contact, Satir (1976)
Conjoint Family Therapy, Satir (1983)
Satir: Step by Step, Satir & Baldwin (1983)
The New Peoplemaking, Satir (1988)

The essence of Virginia Satir's work lies in enhancing the self-esteem of individuals in a family while concomitantly affecting change in the interpersonal system. The model of family therapy developed by Satir has been known by various names throughout its evolution: conjoint family therapy, process therapy, and human validation process model. It is considered a seminal model that is typically associated with various approaches under the communication as well as the experiential family therapy classification.

Virginia Satir was raised on a farm in Wisconsin. At an early age she decided to be a detective of parents. The following passage provides insight into how Satir's personality and early development presaged some basic themes in her professional work:

> When I was 5, I decided to become a children's detective on parents. There was so much that went on between my parents that made little or no sense to me. Making sense of things around me, feeling loved, and being competent were my paramount concerns. I did feel loved, and felt I was competent, but making sense of all the contradictions, deletions, and distortions I observed both in my parents' relationship and among people outside in the world was heart-rending and confusion-making to me. Sometimes this situation raised questions about my being loved, but mostly it affected my ability to predict, to see clearly, and to develop my total being. (Satir, 1982, pp. 13-14)

After earning a bachelor's degree at the University of Wisconsin, Satir began her professional career as a teacher. She subsequently earned a master's degree in psychiatric social work from the University of Chicago and began a private practice in Chicago in 1951. This private practice was the beginning of Satir's pioneering work with families. In 1955, Satir began to conceptualize her clinical experience into theory while teaching family therapy at the Illinois State Psychiatric Institute.

Prior to her death in 1988, Satir had devoted much of her professional life to private practice, writing, teaching, and international relations. Known for her personal charisma and her unshakable belief in people, Satir is widely acclaimed as one of the pioneers in family therapy. The work of Virginia Satir continues to be promoted by the Avanta Network, an association composed of human service providers who worked and trained in Satir's model (Horne & Passmore, 1991).

HISTORICAL INFLUENCES

Evidence of early training in Freudian psychoanalysis is apparent in Satir's model, although she rejected the essence of deterministic Freudian thought. Also, reviewers have noted similarities between Satir's model, Adler's holistic orientation, and Jung's position on the possibility of personality integration (Satir & Bitter, 1991). Parallels between Satir and Carl Rogers include the belief in the inherent goodness and growth tendency in humans, the importance of self-worth, and an emphasis on congruence. The systemic aspect of Satir's theory was most directly influenced by individuals in the Palo Alto group, particularly Gregory Bateson and Don Jackson. Satir cofounded the Mental Research Institute in Palo Alto with Jules Riskin.

Satir's willingness to explore new ideas led to a cross-fertilization of approaches that is evident in her model. Her involvement with the Esalen Institute beginning in 1963 allowed for exposure to a wide range of ideas. The influence of a diverse group of individuals on her theory and therapeutic style is acknowledged by Satir (1982). Among those who influenced Satir's work were Fritz Perls (Gestalt therapy), Eric Berne (transactional analysis), J. L. Moreno (psychodrama), Robert Assigioli (psychosynthesis), George Downing (body therapies), Ida Rolf (life-posturing reintegration), Alex Lowen (bioenergetics), and Milton Erickson (hypnosis).

PHILOSOPHY

The basic philosophy behind the communication/validation family therapy model begins with the idea that humans have an innate growth tendency. All behavior is oriented toward growth "no

matter how distorted [behavior] may look" (Satir, 1983, p. 24). 現視
Satir conceptualized the self as the core of the "human mandala"
and saw individual growth and access to life experience as occurring through the eight aspects of the mandala: physical body, intellect, emotions, the five senses, social needs, nutritional needs, life
space needs, and spiritual needs. Satir also embraced a holistic
view of humans that emphasized the interaction of the body, mind,
and feelings. In Satir and Bitter (1991), Satir notes:

> Once I began to get inklings that the body, mind, and feelings
> formed a triad, I began to see that if what one feels is not
> matched by what one says, the body responds as if it has been
> attacked. The result is physical dysfunction accompanied by
> either disturbances of emotion or thought. (p. 20)

When, as in Satir's model, humans and the social and organi-
zational systems of which they are a part are viewed as holistic systems, components of the system can be conceptualized as
continually interacting to form a dynamic whole. Other characteristics of a systems perspective also apply to Satir's model.

These characteristics include two other components basic to
Satir's philosophy. First, rules have an impact on the effectiveness
of family functioning by influencing roles, communication
processes, and responses to stress. And second, an awareness of
experience in the here and now allows for growth to occur in individual and family systems.

THEORETICAL TENETS

Self-esteem is a core concept in Satir's model and refers to the
meaning and value people associate with the whole of their personal mandala. Individual self-esteem affects both individual
behavior and the interactions among members of a system. There
is a correlation between self-esteem and communication (e.g., low
self-esteem is associated with poor communication).

Communication is the major factor influencing relationships
with others and ourselves. All communication (sending and receiving) is learned and can be unlearned. "Communication and
self-worth are the foundation of the family system" (Satir &
Bitter, 1991, p. 42). Five communication roles or styles exist in

Satir's model. Each role is characterized by a particular style of communication:

❖ *blamer:* engages in fault-finding, name-calling, and criticism.

❖ *computer:* engages in extreme intellectualizing with a paucity of affective content. (Also termed rational role.)

❖ *distractor:* frequently produces irrelevant verbalizations that serve to focus attention away from the issue at hand. (Also termed irrelevant role.)

❖ *placator:* engages in apologetic, tentative, and self-effacing communication that is designed to please others.

❖ *leveler/congruent:* engages in honest, direct, clear communication with affect that is congruent with the content of the message. (Also termed congruent role.)

The leveler style of communication is most effective, and facilitating movement toward this type of communication is a significant aspect of Satir's model.

Congruence is a term used to describe both a style of communication and a way of being for a person. Congruence involves using words that accurately match personal feelings and experience so that communication and meta-communication match and there are no double-bind messages. As a state of being, a congruent person is alert, balanced, and in touch with personal resources:

> Anything can be talked about: anything can be commented on; any question can be raised; there is nothing to hold back. (Satir, Stachowiak, & Taschman, 1975, p. 49)

Incongruence denotes the antithesis of congruence. Incongruence is a type of communication in which the verbal and nonverbal components do not match. As a state of being, incongruence is concomitant with distress and dysfunction in the individual and the family system. Examples of incongruent communication are:

❖ incomplete communication,

❖ assumptions,

❖ ambiguous communication, and

❖ double messages.

FUNCTIONAL AND DYSFUNCTIONAL EFFECTS ON FAMILIES

In *Conjoint Family Therapy* (1983), Satir notes that families are held together by mutually reinforcing functions. These functions are:

❖ to provide a sexual experience for the mates;

❖ to contribute to the continuity of the race by producing and nurturing children;

❖ to cooperate economically by dividing labor between the adults according to sex, convenience, and precedents, and between adults and children according to the child's age and sex;

❖ to maintain a boundary (by the incest taboo) between the generations so that smooth task-functioning and stable relationships can be maintained;

❖ to transmit culture to the children by parental teaching;

❖ to recognize when one of the members is no longer a child but has become an adult capable of performing adult roles and functions; and

❖ to provide for the eventual care of parents by their children.

Among these functions, transmission of culture is perhaps the most complex. Parents must teach children roles or socially accepted ways to act with others in different social situations, and these roles vary according to the age and sex of the child. Parents also teach the child how to cope with the inanimate environment, how to communicate, how to use words and gestures so that they will have a generally accepted meaning for others, and how and when to express emotions, generally guiding the child's emotional reactivity. The family teaches the child by appealing to his or her love and fear and by communicating to the child verbally, nonverbally, and by example.

In functional families, all of these functions of families are fulfilled. This is achieved by clear communication in the family system, effective roles, and having family rules that are few in number, reasonable, relevant, flexible, and consistently applied.

Satir and Bitter (1991) provide this description of a functional family:

> Functional family process and personal maturation are characterized by many of the same aspects: an openness to change, flexibility of response, the generation of personal choices or system option, an awareness of resources, and appreciation for difference as well as similarity, equality in relationships, personal responsibility, reasonable risk, freedom of experience and expression, clarity, and congruent communication. (p. 25)

This description of a functional family is compatible with Satir's depiction of an "open system"—a clear interchange of information and resources within and without the system that is adaptive and dynamic. The functional family system will operate effectively within the context of larger systems (e.g., social, cultural).

A dysfunctional family has characteristics of a "closed system"—poor interchange of information and resources within and without the system that is maladaptive and rigid. The presence of dysfunction in one family member (or "pain" as Satir prefers to call it) is symptomatic of dysfunction in one of the larger systems, usually the family. Since all families have problems, the difficulties themselves and the ensuing stress are not the "problem"; coping is the problem. Dysfunctional family systems are unable to cope effectively because they have rules that are fixed, arbitrary, and inconsistently applied. These rules tend to maintain the status quo and may serve to bolster parent self-esteem. Ultimately a dysfunctional system loses its ability to cope and can become chaotic. A depiction of this type of process is provided by Walsh (1980):

> The sequence begins with an incident between family members or between the family and the outside world. This incident causes stress in the unit and unbalances the delicate homeostasis that exists. Some resolution of the incident must be achieved in order to lower the stress and balance the system. A healthy family will use good communication methods in order to achieve a functional resolution of the conflict. An unhealthy family, lacking effective communication methods, will not resolve the incident in a functional way. Lacking this resolution they must then transmit the stress to the identified patient [IP]. This individual will eventually develop symptoms, and he will carry the dysfunction for the entire family. The crucial point in this sequence of events is the attempted resolution of a problem using either good or faulty

communication methods. Faulty methods lead directly to dysfunction, which is expressed in the IP. Therefore, the remediation of individual problem behavior is focused entirely on the family communication process. (p. 12)

Figure 2.1 provides a visual depiction of the process that produces a dysfunctional system.

ASSESSMENT AND DIAGNOSIS

Assessment occurs simultaneously with therapy. Symptoms that bring families into therapy are always framed within a relational perspective; "any symptom signals a blockage in growth and has a survival connection to a system which requires blockage and distortion of growth in some form in all of its members to keep its balance" (Satir, 1982, p. 12).

Entering into the family process is the first step in assessment. Gathering information about the family directly by asking questions or by observing the dynamics of the family is an overriding concern in the assessment process. Defining the major triadic relationships in the system and uncovering the roles, rules, and communication processes in the family are also key elements of family diagnosis. Examining the relationship messages (frequently communicated nonverbally and at a low level of conscious awareness) as well as the content component of communication with a family in the here and now of a session is of paramount importance.

Although Satir does not have a standard procedure for assessing families, some of the interventions we describe in the techniques section further the assessment process (e.g., family life chronology, family map, and sculptures).

GOALS OF TREATMENT

The outcome of family therapy in general terms is stated quite clearly by Satir (1983) as follows:

Treatment is completed:
- When family members can complete transactions, check, and ask for feedback.

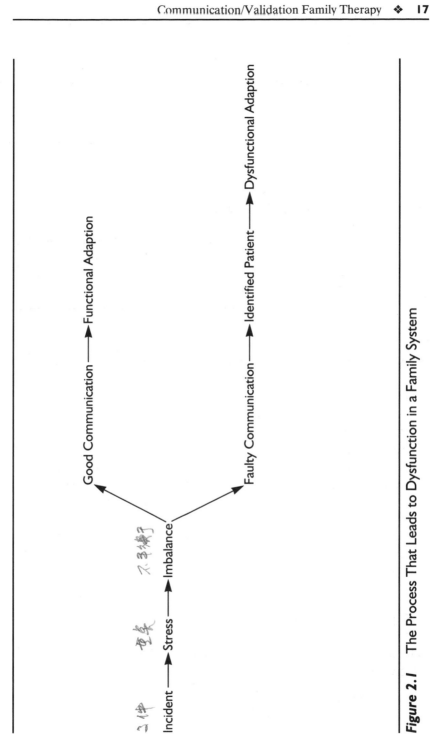

Figure 2.1 The Process That Leads to Dysfunction in a Family System

open + reduce conflict

- When they can interpret hostility.
- When they can see how others see them.
- When one member can tell another how he/she manifests him/herself.
- When one member can tell another what he/she hopes, fears, and expects from him/her.
- When they can disagree.
- When they can make choices.
- When they can learn through practice.
- When they can free themselves from harmful effects of past models.
- When they can give a clear message, that is, be congruent in their behavior, with a minimum of difference between feelings and communication, and with a minimum of hidden messages. (p. 176)

A focus on the process of goal attainment is provided by Satir and Baldwin (1983). The first goal is to instill hope and encouragement in family members. Accessing, enhancing, and creating coping skills is the second goal. The third goal involves facilitating growth-oriented movement in the family beyond simple symptom relief by releasing and directing energy that was previously tied up in symptomatic behaviors.

goals

In short, the general goal of family therapy in this model is to facilitate growth in the family and between its members in terms of self-esteem and effective communication. Other goals of family therapy could involve movement toward the specific desired changes particular to each unique family.

TREATMENT PROCESS

The treatment process in the communication/validation model is consistent with the goals of treatment in that family work is a process of facilitating effective communication in a rational context. Five common stages of the treatment process are usually followed regardless of the specific presenting issues:

1. Establish trust with the family. Develop an assessment and treatment plan early to gain the confidence of the family.

2. Develop awareness through experience. The therapist helps the family develop new awarenesses about their functioning by asking specific questions or using specific techniques (see techniques section).

3. Create new understandings in family members through new or increased awareness of their family dynamics.

4. Have family members express and apply these new understandings through different behaviors during the session.

5. Have family members use the new behaviors outside the therapeutic environment.

Satir and Bitter (1991) note that with each successful cycle of the change process, the family feels less anxious and movement through the stages becomes easier. Eventually the family may come to see change as an expected part of life.

TECHNIQUES

The family therapist is part of the process of facilitating a family's growth in therapy. Consequently, it is crucial that the therapist be grounded in his or her skills, experiences, and sense of well-being when using these techniques with a family. Many of Satir's interventions arose spontaneously out of her observations and intuitions regarding families in the therapeutic moment. The following twelve techniques are common in communication/validation therapy sessions.

1. *Family life fact chronology.* A holistic family history is made extending from the birth of the oldest grandparents to the present.

2. *Family maps.* Visual representations are created of family structure over three generations, similar to genograms. In Satir's use of this technique, three family maps are drawn: mother's family of origin, father's family of origin, and the current family.

3. *Ropes.* The binds and pulls of ropes are used in the session to provide concrete representations of the dynamics in the family system.

4. *Sculpture.* A physical arrangement of the members of a family is made, with the placement of each person determined by an individual family member (or therapist) acting as "director"; the resulting tableau represents that person's symbolic view of family relationships (Goldenberg & Goldenberg, 1991). All entities that affect the family dynamics (including pets, extended family, friends) are symbolically brought into the sculpture through the use of role playing and fantasy (Satir & Bitter, 1991).

5. *Drama.* Enactments of significant events in the family's history can provide an opportunity for a new perspective and for more insight.

6. *Family reconstruction.* Similar to the use of drama, family reconstruction involves enactment of events from the family history based on information derived from the family life fact chronology or family maps.

7. *Reframing.* The therapist creates a shift in the perceptions of family members. "The therapist decreases threat of blame by accentuating the idea of puzzlement and the idea of good intentions" (Satir, 1983, p. 142).

8. *Humor.* Humor can be used to promote contact (between therapist and family as well as among family members), mitigate intensity, clarify or exaggerate a dynamic, and encourage movement in a way that decreases defensive reactions.

9. *Verbalizing presuppositions.* The therapist overtly states presuppositions that are evident in a family's behavior. For example, Satir would verbalize the hope and expectation for change a family manifests by virtue of their involvement in therapy.

10. *Denominalization.* This involves obtaining specific behavioral descriptions for words such as love and respect and discovering exactly what must be done for the person to perceive that he or she is receiving respect. The clarified answer is often related to the individual's primary sensory-based representational system (i.e., visual, auditory, or kinesthetic) (Woods & Martin, 1984).

11. *Anchoring.* Anchoring is the learned association between a stimulus and a response or between one response and another.

When the stimulus or initiating response is triggered, the associated response will be elicited (Dilts & Green, 1982). This technique serves to bring feelings to the level of interpersonal physical experience. Woods and Martin (1984) provide an example of how Satir might have used this technique with a marital couple:

> Satir might ask her to look at her husband and "feel what she feels." When a positive response becomes evident in the individual (i.e., altered breathing, tear), Satir would touch her shoulder gently at the peak of positive emotion. Apparently this helps connect the particular emotion with the touch which makes the feeling more concrete for the individual. (p. 10)

12. *Multiple family therapy.* With this technique, numerous unrelated families are brought together for joint family sessions.

ROLE OF THE THERAPIST

The primary role of the therapist in the communication/validation model is to serve as a guide to the family through the process of change. Given this, the therapist should:

❖ create a comfortable, threat-free environment in the sessions such that families can take the risk of looking at their behavior;

❖ structure the therapeutic process and set the rules for interaction to decrease threat and create a safe therapeutic environment;

❖ allay individual and family defenses by interpreting anger as hurt or by explaining that pain is an acceptable and expressible feeling in therapy;

❖ educate clients about their roles to increase self-control and accountability;

❖ complete gaps or interpret communication, particularly when incongruence exists between the content and the relationship messages (e.g., acknowledging a person's tense body language even though the person says he or she has no anger toward another family member); and

❖ model effective communication, especially personal congruence.

Despite this list of "shoulds" for therapists, Satir asserts the primary importance of the therapist's self in the change process:

> In this role, the therapist's personhood and humanness [are] more important than any particular set of skills. Faith in the ability of people and in systems to grow and change is essential. (Satir & Bitter, 1991, p. 29)

Satir's presence in therapy sessions in the role of therapist is legendary. She was particularly known for her warmth, personal power, and frequent use of touch and activity.

EVALUATION OF THE HUMAN VALIDATION PROCESS MODEL

Similar to other models of family therapy, the efficacy of the communication/validation model has been evaluated primarily on the basis of clinical experience. Satir herself saw more than 5,000 families during her career and reported high rates of success. Research findings relevant to Satir's model include the following studies.

The Family Research Project (Winter, 1989) examined the effectiveness of therapists using the models of Satir, Bowen, and Haley. Satir's practitioners began with 59 families, and 57 of them completed therapy (97%). Multiple measures of effectiveness of therapy and family change supported the efficacy of the communication/validation model. This study also revealed that families treated in multiple family groups tended to improve more than families seen only as a family unit.

Indirect support for the clinical efficacy of the communication/validation model is provided by Gurman and Kniskern (1986). In their review of the literature on family therapy outcome research, they conclude that:

> The only treatment ingredients that have received consistently positive empirical support as facilitating the outcomes of marital therapies apparently regardless of the general mode of such therapies (cf. Gurman, 1975; Jacobson, 1979) are those that increase couples' communication skills (Birchler, 1979; Gurman &

Kniskern, 1977, 1978; Jacobson, 1978, 1979). In fact, at this point, it is defensible to argue that increased communication skills, however they are achieved, are a sine qua non of effective marital therapy. (p. 749)

Gurman and Kniskern (1986) caution that this finding should not be construed as stating that improved communication is sufficient for positive outcomes in most cases. Nevertheless, this finding bodes well for the model in light of Satir's emphasis on facilitating clear, congruent communication within the family.

Cottone (1992) provides an evaluation of Satir's theory as being "theoretically deficient" (p. 209). This criticism is based on his position that Satir was unsuccessful in her attempt to integrate intrapsychic and interpersonal concepts into a theoretically consistent model. Despite this criticism, Cottone acknowledges the major contribution Satir made to the field of family therapy.

REFERENCES

Cottone, R. R. (1992). *Theories and paradigms of counseling and psychotherapy.* Boston: Allyn and Bacon.

Dilts, R., & Green, J. D. (1982). Applications of neurolinguistic programming in family therapy. In A. M. Horne & M. M. Ohlsen (Eds.), *Family counseling and therapy* (pp. 214–244). Itasca, IL: F. E. Peacock.

Goldenberg, I., & Goldenberg, H. (1991). *Family therapy: An overview.* Pacific Grove, CA: Brooks/Cole.

Gurman, A. S., & Kniskern, D. P. (Eds.). (1986). *Handbook of family therapy* (2nd ed.). New York: Brunner/Mazel.

Horne, A. M., & Passmore, J. L. (1991). *Family counseling and therapy* (2nd ed.). Itasca, IL: F. E. Peacock.

Satir, V. (1972). *Peoplemaking.* Palo Alto, CA: Science and Behavior Books.

Satir, V. M. (1976). *Making contact.* Millbrae, CA: Celestial Arts.

Satir, V. M. (1982). The therapist and family therapy: Process model. In A. M. Horne & M. M. Ohlsen (Eds.), *Family counseling and therapy.* Itasca, IL: F. E. Peacock.

Satir, V. M. (1983). *Conjoint family therapy* (3rd ed.). Palo Alto, CA: Science and Behavior Books. (Original work published 1964; 2nd ed., 1967).

Satir, V. M. (1988). *The new peoplemaking.* Palo Alto, CA: Science and Behavior Books.

Satir, V. M., & Baldwin, M. (1983). *Satir: Step by step.* Palo Alto, CA: Science and Behavior Books.

Satir, V. M., & Bitter, J. R. (1991). Human validation process model. In A. M. Horne & J. L. Passmore (Eds.), *Family counseling and therapy* (2nd ed.). Itasca, IL: F. E. Peacock.

Satir, V. M., Stachowiak, J., & Taschman, H. A. (1975). *Helping families to change.* New York: Tiffany.

Walsh, W. (1980). *A primer of family therapy.* Springfield, IL: Charles C Thomas.

Winter, J. (1989). *Family research project: Treatment outcomes and results.* Unpublished manuscript, the Family Institute of Virginia, Richmond.

Woods, M. D., & Martin, D. (1984). The work of Virginia Satir: Understanding her theory and technique. *American Journal of Family Therapy, 12*(4), 3–11.

Bowenian Theory

❖ **MAJOR THEORIST: Murray Bowen** ❖

PRIMARY SOURCES FOR FURTHER READING

Family Therapy in Clinical Practice, Bowen (1978)
The Bowen Family Theory and Its Uses, Hall (1981)
Family Evaluation: An Approach Based on Bowen Theory,
    Kerr & Bowen (1988)
Bowen Family Systems Theory, Papero (1990)

Bowenian theory has been described as having the most comprehensive view of human behavior and human problems of any approach to family treatment (Nichols & Schwartz, 1991). The primary emphasis in this model is to provide a theory of family functioning. The model of therapy derived from this theory is a secondary concern. Relative to other models of family therapy, Bowenian theory tends to have a more intellectual orientation and less of an emotional or experiential focus.

Bowenian theory was originally formulated by Murray Bowen and was referred to by the name family systems theory. Because family systems theory was sometimes confused with general systems theory, that name was abandoned and the name Bowenian theory replaced it. It is a first generation family therapy model.

Trained as a physician, Murray Bowen elected to specialize in psychiatry. During his residency at the Menninger Clinic, Bowen became increasingly dissatisfied with psychoanalytic concepts that were not amenable to validation by conventionally accepted scientific methods. Consequently, Bowen began to develop a new theory characterized as "a natural systems theory, designed to fit precisely with the principles of evolution and the human as an evolutionary being" (Kerr & Bowen, 1988, p. 360). Refinement of Bowenian theory continued after his move to the National Institute for Mental Health (NIMH) in Bethesda, Maryland, in 1954. At the NIMH, Bowen had entire families admitted to the psychiatric research ward. Research with these families was directed by Bowenian theory, and the theory was extended and modified when practitioners were confronted with new or incompatible information. During his five years at NIMH, the focus of Bowen's research was on families with schizophrenic offspring, particularly the symbiotic relationship observed between mothers and their children. Eventually, however, the theory evolved to include the entire family and addressed other types of families as well. As Bowen (1978) states:

> Since that time the effort has been to extend the theoretical orientation from a family concept of schizophrenia to a family theory of emotional illness and to adapt the family psychotherapy to the entire range of emotional illness. (p. 105)

In 1959, Bowen moved to the school of medicine at Georgetown University. Further development of his theory occurred at

Georgetown, and in 1968 a postgraduate training program in family therapy was initiated by Bowen. At the Georgetown University Family Center work continues on Bowenian theory and its therapeutic application. Murray Bowen died in 1990. Prominent figures in Bowenian theory include Michael Kerr, Daniel Papero, Philip Guerin, and Thomas Fogerty.

HISTORICAL INFLUENCES

The emphasis on scientific rigor is salient in Bowen's work. The natural sciences and the concept of evolution served as models for Bowen's concept of psychology as a science. Charles Darwin and Sigmund Freud had a significant impact on Bowen's thinking. Many concepts in Bowenian theory are descended from psychoanalytic thought. Bowen himself was in analysis for 13 years.

As opposed to being based on general systems theory, which emphasizes feedback mechanisms and self-regulating systems, Bowen's model is closer to natural systems theory. Natural systems theory suggests that the family, like all systems (e.g., ant colonies, tides, or the solar system), is guided by processes common in nature (Goldenberg & Goldenberg, 1991).

PHILOSOPHY

Bowenian theory is rooted in the idea that humans have a common evolutionary heritage at primitive levels of functioning that has an impact on behavior (e.g., reflexive and reactive emotional responses). This aspect of functioning is universal and transcends historical and cultural contexts.

Two counterbalancing life forces are relevant to family functioning (Papero, 1991): individuality, a natural force rooted in an instinctual drive to be a self-contained independent organism; and togetherness, a natural force rooted in an instinctual need for others and a sense of being connected to another person or a group. These forces are pervasive in that all relationships have a dynamic interplay of individuality and togetherness.

Humans have both emotional systems and intellectual systems. When these systems operate in a separate but harmonious manner, the individual has a choice between reacting in an emotional fashion and reacting in an intellectual fashion in any given situation. When anxiety escalates emotional intensity, the intellectual and emotional systems become fused. Consequently, thinking and behavior become more emotionally determined and choice is compromised.

The family is an emotionally interdependent unit. A change in one part of the family system will evoke changes in other parts and in the entire family. However, behaviors in a family tend to crystallize in regular patterns through time. These patterns are frequently repeated in several generations. Families exert a strong influence to promote the conformity of each member's behavior (i.e., homeostasis). The family establishes the emotional climate and behaviors that members will recreate in nonfamily settings.

Bowenian theory can be applied to other kinds of social groups, including those involved with work, religion, and politics. These groups manifest emotional processes similar to those of the family unit.

THEORETICAL TENETS

Eight major concepts constitute the core of Bowenian theory. These interrelated concepts build on the cornerstone of the theory, the emotional system.

> It [the emotional system] includes the force that biology defines as instinct, reproduction, the automatic activity controlled by the autonomic nervous system, subjective emotional and feeling states and the forces that govern relationship systems. . . . In broad terms, the emotional system governs the "dance of life" in all living things. (Bowen, 1975, p. 380)

Another key term in early Bowenian work is "undifferentiated family ego mass." This refers to the intense emotional oneness in a family that causes emotionality that interferes with thinking and prevents the individual's differentiation from the family (Bowen, 1978). Hall notes that Bowen no longer uses this terminology (the term *fusion* is currently preferred), yet the eight core concepts were based in part on this term (Hall, 1981). The eight core concepts of Bowenian theory are:

1. *Differentiation of self.* In the context of an emotional system, this is the relative degree of autonomy an individual maintains while remaining in meaningful relationships with others. Highly differentiated individuals have a more fully integrated, solid self (concept of self that is non-negotiable with others), and behavior is guided primarily by the intellect. Individuals with low levels of differentiation are guided predominantly by their pseudo-self (i.e., a concept of self that is negotiable with others), and behavior tends to be directed by their emotions.

2. *Triangles.* A triangle is the basic unit of interdependence in the family emotional system. When anxiety in a dyad reaches a certain level, a third person is predictably drawn into the emotional field of the twosome. Triangles in a family may lay dormant and not be overtly apparent, yet these triangles can be activated during times of stress. In general, the higher the fusion in a family, the greater the efforts to triangulate to relieve tension. The least differentiated person in the system is the most vulnerable to being triangulated.

3. *Nuclear family emotional process.* This concept describes the range of relationship patterns in the system between parents and children. There are four mechanisms used by the family to manage anxiety when it becomes too intense in the nuclear family. All four mechanisms may be employed, but a family may predominantly use one or perhaps more:

   ❖ *emotional distance.* In a fused family system with high levels of anxiety a family member may increase interpersonal distance when he or she is unable to manage emotional reactivity (Bowen, 1978). Frequently this can result in more distance than the individual actually desires.

   ❖ *marital conflict.* The amount of conflict in a marriage is typically a function of the degree of fusion in the relationship and the intensity of the underlying anxiety (Papero, 1991). A cyclic process may occur in which conflict is followed by emotional distance, a period of warm togetherness, then an increase in tension that precipitates another conflict and the perpetuation of the cycle.

❖ *transmission of the problem to a child.* Problems and anxiety between spouses can be avoided by parental focus on one or more children. The most common pattern is for the mother to focus much of her emotional energy on a child while the father supports this via reciprocal distancing. The focused-on child has increased reactivity and fusion of intellect and emotion and is most vulnerable to the development of problems.

❖ *dysfunction in a spouse.* Reciprocal roles may develop in the couple with one member being inadequate or dysfunctional and the other being overly adequate in an effort to compensate. This pattern can increase and solidify to the extent that the low functioning individual develops a chronic mental or physical malady.

4. *Family projection process.* The level of differentiation of the parents is passed on to one or more of their offspring. Typically, one child in a family will have increased emotional involvement with one of the parents. This overinvolvement can range from the parent being excessively solicitous to the parent being extremely hostile. The dynamic impairs the child's capacity to function effectively in social settings. The degree of differentiation of the parents and the level of stress in the family determine the intensity of the family projection process.

5. *Emotional cutoff.* In an attempt to deal with the fusion and lack of differentiation in their intimate relationships, family members or segments of the extended system may distance themselves from each other and become emotionally divorced (Hall, 1981). Although the cut-off individual may appear to handle the relationship with the family, the individual remains more vulnerable to other intense relationships. Kerr (1981) suggests that emotional cutoff indicates a problem (fusion between generations), solves a problem (decreases anxiety associated with family contact), and creates a problem (isolates individuals who could benefit from contact). As a result of the cutoff, the individual remains stuck in the emotional system of the family and may be less able to respond effectively to problem-solving situations. The consequent dysfunction can also manifest itself in other ways such as superficial relationships, physical illness, depression, and impulsive behaviors (Walsh, 1980).

6. *Multigenerational transmission process.* The strong tendency to repeat impairing patterns of emotional behavior in successive generations culminates in lowered levels of differentiation of self for certain members of the younger generations (Hall, 1981). Bowen proposes that individuals at equivalent levels of differentiation find each other and marry and may have one or more children at even lower levels of differentiation. This repetitive pattern results in successively lower levels of differentiation in subsequent generations. The process culminates in an ultimate level of impairment that is consistent with schizophrenia.

7. *Sibling position.* Seniority and sex distribution among siblings in the same and related generations have a strong influence on behavior (Hall, 1981). The research by Walter Toman (1969) describes different roles individuals take as a result of their position in their families of origin (e.g., oldest child, younger sister, youngest child). Bowen suggested that interactive patterns between marital couples could be related to the individuals' respective roles from their families of origin. For example, two oldest children marrying could lead to competition to see who is in charge.

8. *Emotional process in society (societal regression).* The processes characteristic of families can also be observed in interactions on a societal level. For example, with high anxiety and stress due to crime, unemployment, and pollution, there is a societal tendency toward emotional reactivity and a decreased likelihood for individuation through effective use of intellectual processes. Bowen noted that the recent history of our society seems to reflect this type of regression.

FUNCTIONAL AND DYSFUNCTIONAL EFFECTS ON FAMILIES

A functional family is characterized by the viability or survival value of its emotional processes rather than by its form or structure. The viability of the family is also correlated with the family's management of tension between individuality and togetherness forces. Family processes that are flexible allow for differentiation of self of the individual family members. This type of family will be characterized by open communication, a low frequency of symptomatic behaviors, and a lack of emotional cutoff.

In Bowenian theory, family processes that are conducive to the successful adaptation of the family unit are termed "strength" (Hall, 1981). Dysfunction, in Bowenian theory, is termed "weakness," which denotes a low degree of viability of emotional processes. This is destructive to the family, eventually leading to its extinction (Hall, 1981). Dysfunctional processes in a family may be manifested by high levels of emotional intensity, rigid and restrictive relationships (e.g., dependency or isolation), low levels of individual differentiation of self, and overt symptoms in individual family members.

As previously mentioned, Bowen postulates that individuals with similar levels of differentiation tend to seek each other out and marry. Individuals with low levels of differentiation who marry are more likely to have more intense levels of fusion, which leads to the previously described problems. Through the multigenerational process, dysfunction in one generation is passed on to members of the next generation and tends to be perpetuated in this manner.

ASSESSMENT AND DIAGNOSIS

In Bowenian theory, the therapist avoids pathologizing one family member (frequently termed the "identified patient"). Instead, the problem is conceptualized in terms of the entire family system. Assessment begins as information about family processes is collected in the initial sessions. Bowenian therapists may structure the family evaluation in a variety of ways. Kerr (1981, p. 252) offers a general framework for an evaluation interview:

❖ history of the presenting problem,
❖ history of the nuclear family,
❖ history of the husband's extended family system,
❖ history of the wife's extended family system, and
❖ conclusion.

Information that is gathered can be documented on a family genogram that provides a visual depiction of family processes. The genogram, an example of which is presented in Figure 3.1, is readily identified as a key tool in Bowenian theory. Frequently, nodal events (i.e., events subsequent to which family functioning has shifted) such as births, divorces, and deaths are documented on a family genogram. Characteristics of the family system, such as triangles and emotional cutoffs, can be represented so that the multigenerational processes that have shaped the nuclear family can be illuminated. A good source for the construction of a genogram is McGoldrick and Gerson (1985).

The family genogram that is constructed serves as a blueprint that enables the therapist to understand the emotional system. It also functions as a guide to treatment and may be shared with the family as a component of the therapeutic process.

Another term relevant to assessment in Bowenian theory is the *differentiation of self* scale. This rating instrument (Figure 3.2)

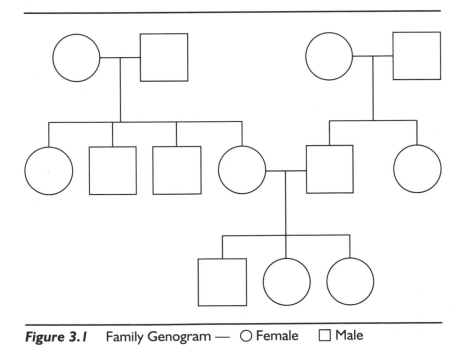

Figure 3.1 Family Genogram — ◯ Female ☐ Male

was developed by Bowen to measure and describe an individual's tendency toward individuality or togetherness in a family. The scale is a continuum representing the range of human functioning from the lowest level of differentiation (a rating of 0) to the highest level (a rating approaching the ideal of 100) (Walsh, 1980).

GOALS OF TREATMENT

The most important goal of Bowenian theory is improved differentiation of the self (Bowen, 1978). With increased differentiation, individual family members are better able to tolerate anxiety and access their intellectual functions. Decreased emotional reactivity and enhanced intellectual functioning are achieved through the attainment of other goals of treatment in this model:

> A goal in family therapy is to reduce the level of anxiety, to improve the level of responsible open communication within the family, and to reduce the irresponsible, underground communication of secrets and gossip to others. (Bowen, 1978, p. 291)

Another goal of treatment is to decrease the emotional cutoff and work to resolve unfinished business with the family of origin.

In the Bowenian model, therapists have goals of treatment for themselves that are crucial to the family's attainment of their goals (Kerr & Bowen, 1988). These goals include:

❖ reduced anxiety in the emotional field to improve the functional level of differentiation of self and reduce symptoms, and

❖ improve the basic level of differentiation to increase the adaptability of the person to intense emotional fields.

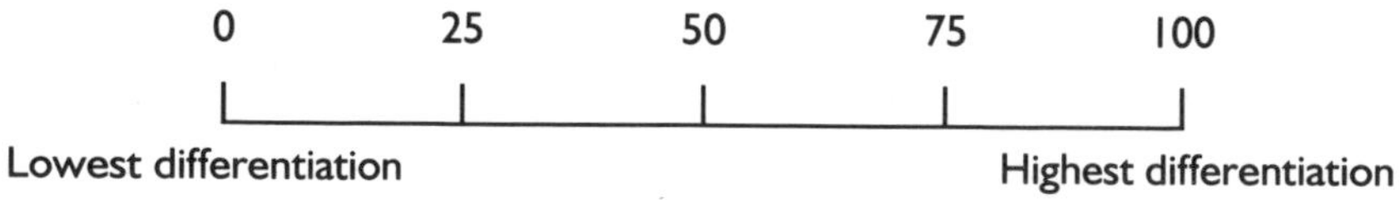

| 0 | 25 | 50 | 75 | 100 |

Lowest differentiation   Highest differentiation

Figure 3.2   Differentiation Scale

Symptom reduction and decreased anxiety can occur relatively quickly in treatment (i.e., from several sessions to several months of treatment); improvement in the basic level of differentiation is a long-term process that can take a number of years.

TREATMENT PROCESS

A primary concern in the treatment process is stated by Bowen as follows:

> Progress in therapy depends on the therapist's ability to relate meaningfully to the family without becoming emotionally entangled in the family system. (1978, p. 312)

Bowen has listed five main functions of the therapist in the treatment process with a family (Papero, 1991, p. 61):

❖ define and clarify the relationship between spouses (develop and use the genogram),

❖ keep self detriangled from the family emotional system,

❖ teach the functioning of emotional systems using the tenets of the model,

❖ demonstrate differentiation by managing self during the course of therapy, and

❖ resolve cutoffs.

Kerr and Bowen (1988) suggest using the following questions in the process:

❖ Who initiated the therapy?

❖ What is the symptom and which family member or family relationship is symptomatic?

❖ What is the immediate relationship system (this usually means the nuclear family) of the symptomatic person?

❖ What are the patterns of emotional functioning in the nuclear family?

❖ What is the intensity of the emotional process in the nuclear family?

❖ What influences that intensity—an overload of stressful events or a low level of adaptiveness?

❖ What is the nature of the extended family systems, particularly in terms of their stability and availability?

❖ What is the degree of emotional cutoff from each extended family system?

❖ What is the prognosis?

❖ What are important directions for therapy?

If the therapist remains detriangled and the family is able to interact in an atmosphere of low anxiety and reactivity, progress will occur. Bowen describes the successful treatment process as follows:

> After the family anxiety subsides and the spouses are more capable of reflection, individuality forces begin to surface in one spouse. This occurs as the spouse begins to focus more on the part the self plays in the relationship problems, to decrease blaming of the other for one's own discomfort and unhappiness, and to accept responsibility for changing self. (1978, p. 315)

The therapist may work with a marital couple, the entire family, or just one individual from the family. The configuration of individuals seen by the therapist may change as treatment progresses.

TECHNIQUES

Bowenian theory is not technique-oriented relative to other models of family therapy. Instead, the therapist has a focus on understanding the family's emotional process while remaining detriangled. Despite this, certain techniques are frequently employed to advance the therapeutic process. One technique, used to keep emotional reactivity and anxiety in the sessions low, is having family members speak to the therapist as opposed to having them speak directly to one another. Another useful technique is to focus on thinking and intellectual processes by asking frequent factual questions. Externalize the thinking of family members such that members of the family system can hear each other's perspective.

The Bowenian therapist remains emotionally neutral and avoids taking sides; therefore the therapist remains detriangled from the family emotional system. The therapist also maintains emotional neutrality in the session through the use of modeling, nonverbal behavior, and the appropriate use of humor (Bowen, 1978). This can lead to a reduction of fusion and emotional cutoffs in the system.

When appropriate (i.e., after anxiety has subsided), didactic teaching is used to provide a cognitive framework to which the family can refer to understand problems and the treatment process. The intent is to help individuals in a family increase their awareness of their roles in the family systems process.

Genograms are used to organize information about a family (e.g., triangles, relationship processes) and provide a means to track the family's progress in therapy. And resolution of cutoffs is often facilitated by the use of grief or loss therapy techniques (e.g., journaling, letter writing, empty chair).

Multiple family therapy is employed to enhance the learning of a family by having them observe the emotional processes of other families in therapy. In Bowen's use of this technique, families meet together as a group, and the therapist works with one family at a time while the other families observe.

ROLE OF THE THERAPIST

The primary task of the therapist is to remain removed from the family emotional process. The therapist closely observes the process of communication, gains an understanding of the family dynamics, and creates an atmosphere in the session where work toward differentiation can occur. By maintaining the "I-Position" (i.e., holding to one's position based on thinking rather than emotion despite the emotional pressures from the family), the therapist enables the family to touch on important issues and elicits calm, thoughtful responses (Bowen, 1978).

Bowen pioneered the practice of family therapists, addressing their own issues by increasing their differentiation from their families of origin. This personal work by the therapist fosters decreased reactivity when dealing with families and an increased ability to remain detached.

EVALUATION OF THE BOWENIAN MODEL

Bowenian theory is a good example of a working theory because research continues to expand both theory and application. Currently, various staff members at the Family Center at Georgetown University are using this model to guide their work with AIDS, cancer, and other challenging human concerns (Papero, 1991). Extrapolation of Bowenian theory to societal processes is another current area of study, along with work to link family systems with other sciences.

Evidence of the clinical efficacy of Bowenian theory has been based primarily on clinical observation and experience because of Bowen's focus on integrating theory and practice and because of the difficulty associated with experimental testing of the theory (Nichols, 1984). When judged on the criteria for a good theory (Combs, 1989), this model fares relatively well. Bowen's theory is viewed as comprehensive, consistent, useful, and elegant (Nichols, 1984). As previously noted, a shortcoming is the paucity of controlled experimentation to validate the theoretical tenets of the model and to assess its clinical efficacy.

Bowen is seen as one of the pioneers in the development of family theory and therapy (Broderick & Schrader, 1981). Bowenian theory has had a significant impact on the field of family therapy by bringing attention to the relevance of the wider kinship network of family functioning. It has also influenced the other models of family therapy, particularly the development of network therapy by Speck and Attneave (Nichols, 1984).

REFERENCES

Bowen, M. (1975). Family therapy after twenty years. In S. Arieti (Ed.), *American handbook of psychiatry*. New York: Basic Books.

Bowen, M. (1978). *Family therapy in clinical practice*. New York: Jason Aronson.

Broderick, C. B., & Schrader, S. S. (1981). The history of professional marriage and family therapy. In A. S. Gurman & D. P. Kniskern (Eds.), *Handbook of family therapy*. New York: Brunner/Mazel.

Combs, A. W. (1989). *A theory of therapy*. Needham Heights, MA: Allyn and Bacon.

Hall, C. M. (1981). *The Bowen family theory and its uses*. New York: Jason Aronson.

Goldenberg, I., & Goldenberg, H. (1991). *Family therapy: An overview* (3rd ed.). Pacific Grove, CA: Brooks/Cole.

Kerr, M. E. (1981). Family systems theory and therapy. In A. A. Gurman & D. P. Kniskern (Eds.), *Handbook of family therapy*. New York: Brunner/Mazel.

Kerr, M. E., & Bowen, M. (1988). *Family evaluation: An approach based on Bowen theory*. New York: W. W. Norton.

McGoldrick, M., & Gerson, R. (1985). *Genograms in family assessment*. New York: W. W. Norton.

Nichols, M. P. (1984). *Family therapy: Concepts and methods*. New York: Gardner Press.

Nichols, M. P., & Schwartz, R. C. (1991). *Family therapy: Concepts and methods* (2nd ed.). Boston: Allyn and Bacon.

Papero, D. V. (1990). *Bowen family systems theory*. Boston: Allyn and Bacon.

Papero, D. V. (1991). The Bowen theory. In A. M. Horne & J. L. Passmore (Eds.), *Family counseling and therapy*. Itasca, IL: F. E. Peacock.

Toman, W. (1969). *Family constellation*. New York: Springer.

Walsh, W. (1980). *A primer of family therapy*. Springfield, IL: Charles C Thomas.

Structural
Family Therapy

 MAJOR THEORIST: Salvador Minuchin ❖

PRIMARY SOURCES FOR FURTHER READING

Families of the Slums, Minuchin, Montalvo, Guerney,
    Rosman, & Schumer (1967)
Families and Family Therapy, Minuchin (1974)
Psychosomatic Families: Anorexia Nervosa in Context,
    Minuchin, Rosman, & Baker (1978)
Family Therapy Techniques, Minuchin & Fishman (1981)
Structural Family Therapy, Umbarger (1983)
Family Healing, Minuchin & Nichols (1993)

Structural family therapy is one of the seminal models of family therapy. It is based on the fundamental concepts underlying general structuralist thought. Structuralism approaches all human phenomena with the intent of identifying the codes that regulate human relationships. No other common name is used for this theory.

Structural family therapy is primarily credited to Salvador Minuchin, a psychiatrist born and raised in Argentina. Minuchin's early life experiences include being raised in a huge extended family of over 200 cousins and many family friends (Minuchin, 1974). This left him with a lasting impression of the social context within which human beings function. Professional experiences that shaped Minuchin's thinking include work with families in Israel, development of a therapy approach for low income/minority families through the Wiltwych School for Boys in New York, family therapy with psychosomatic patients, and involvement with the Philadelphia Child Guidance Clinic (Aponte & Van Deusen, 1981). Minuchin continues to practice family therapy, supervise, and teach. He is the author of numerous articles and books on family therapy.

HISTORICAL INFLUENCES

The influence of Alfred Adler, particularly his focus on the social, goal-oriented aspect of humans, is apparent in structural family therapy. Adler's concepts of family constellation, the positive nature of humans, and the ability of humans to change served as a foundation for Minuchin's basic theoretical formulations. The philosophy of Ortega y Gasset that emphasizes individuals interacting with their environment is reflected in Minuchin's focus on the contextual and environmental influences affecting behavior. And systemic thinking, as developed by anthropologist Gregory Bateson, is also at the foundation of structural family therapy.

Minuchin worked with families in a variety of settings and cultures. His diverse experience with these families and his frustration with traditional psychoanalytic therapy served as a catalyst for his development of a more pragmatic, directive, and problem-oriented form of family intervention. Braulio Montalvo, a psychiatrist with whom Minuchin collaborated at Wiltwych, greatly influenced his theory and clinical style (Minuchin, 1974). Association with other individuals in the field of family therapy, such as Jay Haley and colleagues at the Philadelphia Child Guidance Clinic, further refined the theory and practice of structural family therapy.

PHILOSOPHY

The philosophy behind structural family therapy focuses attention on the present or future. According to this theory the history of the family is manifest in the present, and therefore it is accessible through interventions in the here and now. Further, humans are social creatures and must be viewed holistically within the context of their social systems. Environmental factors are given priority over hereditary factors.

The reciprocal nature of systemic causality (e.g., an individual's behavior influences and is influenced by his or her social system) is acknowledged. And there is an emphasis on process over content (e.g., the "how" of communication is more important than the "what").

Structural family therapy also holds that the family is a microcosm of the social milieu, and functional and dysfunctional behaviors are taught and perpetuated by the family. The whole (family) and the parts (family members) can be properly explained only in terms of the relations that exist between the parts (Lane, 1970).

THEORETICAL TENETS

The family structure is composed of sets of transactions that form a tightly knit fabric and determine the essence of each individual family. These transactions determine how family members relate, and can be verbal or nonverbal, known or unknown. A family's uniqueness is determined by the idiosyncratic repetitive transactions that make up the family's patterns of functioning. These transactions regulate behavior in two ways: A power hierarchy exists that dictates the authority and decision making in the family, and mutual expectations formed by negotiations over time are determined and fulfilled by individuals in the family.

The components of the family's structure that exist to carry out various family tasks are called subsystems. Subsystems can be formed on the basis of generation, interests, or specific family functions. Family members may belong to several subsystems at the same time. The most prominent and important subsystems in the family are:

❖ *Adult subsystem.* Sometimes termed spousal or marital subsystem. This is the component of a family system that typically includes the spousal dyad and teaches the children about intimacy and commitment.

❖ *Parental subsystem.* Usually composed of the parents but may include members of the extended family (e.g., grandmother). The parental subsystem has the major responsibility for proper child rearing, guidance, limit setting, and discipline.

❖ *Sibling subsystem.* Generally includes the children in a family and serves as a child's first peer group. In the sibling subsystem, the child learns negotiation, cooperation, competition, mutual support, and attachment to friends.

Subsystem boundaries are made up of a set of rules that define who participates in the subsystem and how the individuals participate. The nature of the boundaries will have an impact on the functioning of the subsystem as well as on the entire family unit. Minuchin describes three types of boundaries that lie on a continuum from very rigid to very diffuse:

❖ Rigid boundaries permit minimal interaction or communication between subsystems. Individuals may be isolated and forced to function autonomously. Rigid boundaries provide maximum privacy and minimal interaction. The subsystem may become disengaged from the rest of the family.

❖ Clear boundaries promote open communication and privacy such that subsystems can operate freely to fulfill their functions in the family system. These boundaries are essentially a midpoint between the extremes of rigid and diffuse.

❖ Diffuse boundaries are characterized by poorly defined membership and functions. Task completion is rarely accomplished. Diffuse boundaries provide minimal privacy and maximum interaction. Lines of authority and responsibility are not clearly drawn, and family members may be overinvolved with each other.

Another important issue in structural family therapy is adaptation to stress, a concept that refers to the internal and external sources of stress impinging on the family system and how families adapt to tense situations. Every family attempts to adapt to stress in ways that will preserve the integrity of the structure and thereby maintain homeostasis (Colapinto, 1991). Minuchin identifies four sources of stress that affect families directly:

❖ stressful contact of one member with extrafamilial forces (e.g., parent's work difficulties that are brought home and affect other family members),

❖ stressful contact of the whole family with extrafamilial forces (e.g., an economic recession affecting the family's financial resources),

❖ stress at developmental or transitional points in the family (e.g., children leaving home for school, for work, or to establish their own independence), and

❖ stress related to idiosyncratic problems (e.g., presence of a chronically ill family member).

The family evolves in stages of increasing complexity. The pervasive task throughout this process is to blend the diversity of individual growth with the unity of membership in the family system. Minuchin describes four stages of development that occur in many families:

❖ *Couple formation.* The marital dyad form a functional system by negotiating boundaries (e.g., in-law interactions), reconciling divergent lifestyles, and developing rules regarding conflict and cooperation.

❖ *Young children.* The spousal subsystem reorganizes to adapt to the functions requisite of parenthood.

❖ *School age and adolescent children.* The family interacts with the school system, and intrafamily structures are modified to make this adjustment (e.g., homework, extracurricular activities). As the children grow into adolescence, the family deals with issues around peer influences, loss of parental control, and the initial stages of the child's eventual emancipation.

❖ *Grown children.* Parents and grown children who have emancipated modify parent-child interactions to adult-adult interactions.

The family is seen as a living, open system interacting with the environment (Colapinto, 1991). The rules of the family provide structure by which operations can occur that meet the needs of the family members and the family as a whole. Substructures within the family system interact according to rules that serve as boundaries between subsystems. Internal and external stressors necessitate adaptation of the family structure to maintain homeostasis. One predictable type of stressor is the developmental process experienced by most family systems.

FUNCTIONAL AND DYSFUNCTIONAL EFFECTS ON FAMILIES

From a structural perspective, functional and dysfunctional levels are determined by the adequacy of the fit of a family's structural organization to the requirements of operation within the environmental context. A functional family is characterized by transactions that serve to meet the needs of the individuals in the family and the family unit as a whole. Typically, functional families are characterized by structures that are adaptable and well defined.

A dysfunctional family system occurs when a stressor overloads the family's adaptive and coping mechanisms; consequently, family members' needs are not adequately met. Frequently, the stressor is due to the changing conditions associated with the family development process. Rather than modify the family structure to adapt to the stressor, the family increases the rigidity of the pre-existing inadequate structure. The family system's rigidity and inability to complete the necessary developmental task can result in dysfunction. Usually, one family member (the "identified patient") will manifest the symptom for the family and therein serve as the safety valve for the family by expressing system dysfunction (Friesen, 1985).

There are four general classifications of pathology in structural family therapy. But a family may exhibit several overlapping types of pathology. The four general forms of pathology are:

❖ *Pathology of boundaries.* Subsystem boundaries that are too permeable (enmeshed system) or too rigid (disengaged system) interfere with the adaptive transmission of information between subsystems.

❖ *Pathology of alliances.* Intrafamilial relationships that are not conducive to healthy functioning may be formed on the basis of a common interest. The two primary types of alliance pathology are conflict detouring or scapegoating (e.g., a family reduces tension by blaming problems on one family member), and inappropriate cross-generational coalitions (e.g., members of different generations of a family join together against a third member of the family).

❖ *Pathology of triads.* Inherently unstable family arrangements may be formed in which two members side against a third member. These arrangements are also termed *coalitions* (e.g., mother and son against father).

❖ *Pathology of hierarchy.* Here, the functional decision-making hierarchy with parents in charge is subverted by an alternative arrangement (e.g., father and child form the parental subunit excluding mother).

ASSESSMENT AND DIAGNOSIS

The therapist develops working hypotheses regarding family structure based on observations of family interactions. Problems are formulated in ways that are amenable to change. Interventions designed to affect structural change and therein achieve therapy goals are derived from the working hypotheses. Diagnosis is achieved through the structural process of joining, which Minuchin calls an interactional or "structural diagnosis" (Minuchin,

1974). A structural diagnosis is an ongoing, constantly evolving process in structural family therapy and is based on data from six major areas:

❖ The family structure, including its preferred transactional patterns and the alternative patterns available.

❖ The system's flexibility, and its capacity for elaboration and restructuring (e.g., shifting coalitions and subsystems in response to changing circumstances).

❖ The family system's resonance, reflecting its sensitivity to individual members' input (e.g., high sensitivity being enmeshed, low sensitivity being disengaged).

❖ The family life context, examining the sources of stress and support in the family's ecology.

❖ The family's developmental stage and its performance of the tasks appropriate to that stage.

❖ The identified patient's symptoms and the manner in which they are used to maintain the family's preferred transactional patterns.

The information gathered from the structural diagnosis process can be expressed visually in the form of a therapeutic map (see Figures 4.1 and 4.2). The map facilitates the generation of working hypotheses, identifies restructuring techniques that may be effective, and establishes short-term and long-term treatment goals. The map also serves as an ongoing evaluation of the therapeutic process and may be shared with the family at appropriate intervals.

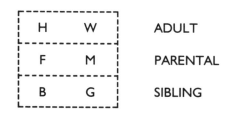

Figure 4.1 Map for Two-Parent Family, Two Children, Clear Boundaries

GOALS OF TREATMENT

The overriding goal of structural family therapy is to solve problems in the family and to change the underlying systemic structure. This goal is achieved through attainment of smaller goals specific to the identified needs as determined by the structural diagnosis

SYMBOLS

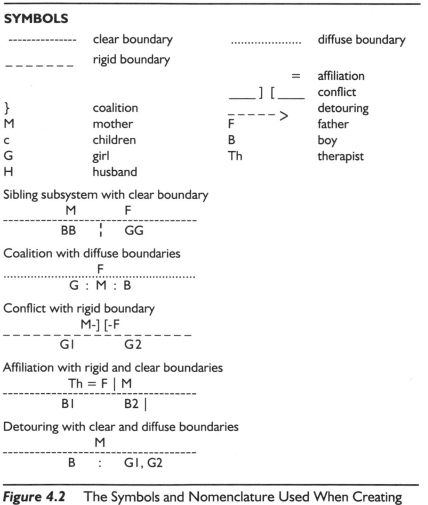

---------------	clear boundary	....	diffuse boundary
_ _ _ _ _ _	rigid boundary		
		=	affiliation
		___] [___	conflict
}	coalition	_ _ _ _ _ >	detouring
M	mother	F	father
c	children	B	boy
G	girl	Th	therapist
H	husband		

Sibling subsystem with clear boundary

```
            M           F
-----------------------------------
       BB   ¦   GG
```

Coalition with diffuse boundaries

```
                F
.....................................
        G  :  M  :  B
```

Conflict with rigid boundary

```
           M-] [-F
_ _ _ _ _ _ _ _ _ _ _ _ _ _ _ _ _
       GI          G2
```

Affiliation with rigid and clear boundaries

```
         Th = F | M
-----------------------------------
       BI          B2 |
```

Detouring with clear and diffuse boundaries

```
               M
-----------------------------------
       B    :   GI, G2
```

Figure 4.2 The Symbols and Nomenclature Used When Creating Therapeutic Maps

Sources: Minuchin, 1974; Walsh, 1980.

and to the particular stage in the therapeutic process (e.g., successfully joining the family in the early stages in therapy).

TREATMENT PROCESS

Minuchin sees treatment as structural change that modifies the family's functioning so it can better perform necessary tasks. Once the therapist has initiated change, the processes will be maintained by the family's self-regulating mechanisms. Since the family is a dynamic system in continual movement, the steps in the therapeutic process may overlap and recycle in "kaleidoscopic sequence" (Minuchin, 1974). Given this caveat, the typical steps in the treatment process of structural family therapy are:

1. *Joining/accommodating.* A process by which a therapist adjusts to the communication style and perceptions of family members to "join" with the system (Minuchin, 1974). The goal in this stage is to establish an effective therapeutic relationship with the family.

2. *Structural diagnosis.* A continuous process of observation and hypothesis testing and reformulation relevant to the family's structure and transactions. A goal in this stage is to provide a framework of information relevant to the problem in the family system that is amenable to structural intervention. Mapping is common in this stage.

3. *Restructuring.* The utilization of therapeutic interventions that bring about change through modification in the family structure. The goal in this stage (and an indicator for termination readiness) is development of a family structure capable of dealing with future stressful situations in appropriate ways.

TECHNIQUES

Techniques in structural family therapy are employed to achieve the goals of the therapeutic process. These techniques can be categorized as either joining or accommodating techniques or restructuring techniques. The following list of techniques is not exhaustive, and Friesen (1985) notes that various techniques from strategic family therapy are often utilized by structural family therapists as well.

Joining or accommodating techniques. The primary goal of joining or accommodating techniques is to establish an effective therapeutic relationship. However, Minuchin considers that these techniques serve a concomitant restructuring function (Walsh, 1980).

❖ *Maintenance.* Supporting specific behaviors or verbalizations to increase the strength and independence of individuals, subsystems, or alliances.

❖ *Tracking.* Using clarification, amplification, and approval of family communication to reinforce individuals and subsystems.

❖ *Mimesis.* Adopting the family's communication style and conforming to its affective range (e.g., if the family frequently uses expletives, the therapist adopts this mode of speaking).

Restructuring techniques. These techniques challenge and unbalance the family system, creating movement that forces the family to seek alternative transactions and solutions.

❖ *Enactment.* Having family members recreate an interaction. The interaction may be relatively innocuous (e.g., planning an outing) or may directly relate to the presenting problems. Enactments are utilized to diagnose family structure, increase intensity, and restructure family systems.

❖ *Actualizing family transactional patterns.* Stimulating naturalistic family interactions so the therapist can observe the typical transactions. This may be achieved by directing the family to have a conversation or by the therapist refusing to answer a question.

❖ *Marking boundaries.* Strengthening diffuse boundaries and increasing the permeability of rigid boundaries to enhance healthy subsystem interaction. This can be accomplished by assisting the family to set new rules, renegotiate old rules, and establish specific functions for each subsystem.

❖ *Escalating stress.* Heightening tension in a family to force them to accept restructuring. This can be achieved by encouraging conflict when it occurs, joining alliances against other family members, and blocking dysfunctional transactional patterns that serve to decrease stress in the system.

❖ *Assigning tasks.* Assigning specific tasks for individuals or subsystems to be accomplished in the session or at home.

❖ *Utilizing symptoms.* Altering the function a symptom serves in the family system by encouraging, deemphasizing, or relabeling the symptom (Minuchin & Fishman, 1981). This may also remove the secondary gain that may be inherent in the symptomology.

❖ *Paradoxical injunction.* Imposing a directive that places the client in a therapeutic double bind that promotes change regardless of client compliance with the directive. Typically utilized when resistance to the directive is anticipated.

❖ *Manipulate mood in the family.* Modeling an exaggerated reflection of a frequently manifested mood in the family. For example, if yelling is frequently used in the family to create a volatile mood, the therapist may yell even louder.

❖ *Support, education, and guidance.* Providing direct instruction to the family to behave differently (e.g., teaching the parents to give more attention to their children).

ROLE OF THE THERAPIST

The therapist joins the system and uses himself or herself to transform it (Minuchin, 1981). The therapist, in the role of expert, is active and directive, determining the structure of the therapy and directing the process. A flexible, diverse personal approach may be utilized to maintain the therapist's freedom of movement and therapeutic leverage. The therapist's personality may be brought into the therapeutic process to further the goals of the family therapy. Minuchin provides an eloquent description of how he integrates his personal style with the techniques and goals of structural family therapy in the sessions:

> As a therapist, I tend to act like a distant relative. I like to tell anecdotes about my own experiences and thinking, and to include

things I have read or heard that are relevant to the particular family. I try to assimilate the family's language and to build metaphors using the family's language and myths. These methods telescope time, investing an encounter between strangers with the affect of an encounter between old acquaintances. They are accommodation techniques, which are vital to the process of joining. (Minuchin, 1974, p. 122)

EVALUATION OF THE STRUCTURAL FAMILY THERAPY MODEL

Structural family therapy has been utilized in the treatment of family and marital problems within a variety of contexts and with diverse presenting concerns. Minuchin has particularly focused on concerns in the family including psychosomatic conditions (primarily anorexia nervosa), physical abuse, divorce, blended families, and alcohol abuse. Available empirical research supports the efficacy of structural family therapy.

Research by Minuchin, Rosman, and Baker (1978) provides empirical support for the structural notion that psychosomatic children regulate stress between parents. This study involved examining the physiological response of children (free fatty acid level in the blood indicating stress) as a result of observing parental conflict.

Outcome research utilizing structural family therapy with families with anorexic children suggested a 90% improvement rate (Minuchin, Rosman, & Baker, 1978). These positive treatment results were maintained at follow-up evaluations of up to two-year intervals (Nichols, 1984).

Research on the application of structural family therapy to the treatment of drug addicts and their families suggested better treatment outcomes compared to individual therapy or a placebo condition (Stanton & Todd, 1979).

The application of structural family therapy to culturally diverse groups was supported when it was found to effect positive change in Hispanic families (Szapocznik et al., 1989). Even though structural family therapy was more effective than psychodynamic child therapy, this research did not support the basic assumption regarding the mechanisms mediating symptom reduction.

Aponte and Van Deusen (1981) provide a summary of research that has been conducted on structural family therapy. They report that this research, despite being in the relatively early stages of development, tends to confirm many of the theoretical tenets of structural family therapy. In their overview of the outcome research based on measures of symptoms and psychosocial change in the index patient, they describe structural family therapy as effective with 73% of the cases and ineffective for the remaining 27% (Aponte & Van Deusen, 1981, p. 357). They add that relative to other studies regarding the effectiveness of family therapy as noted in Gurman and Kniskern (1981), structural family therapy appears to be at least as successful as any other current model of family therapy.

The value of this approach is further evidenced by the impact it has had on other models in the field of family therapy. A recent literature review reveals that components of structural family therapy have been combined with diverse models of therapy including behavioral, strategic, and psychodramatic.

REFERENCES

Aponte, H. J., & Van Deusen, J. M. (1981). Structural family therapy. In A. S. Gurman & D. P. Kniskern (Eds.), *Handbook of family therapy.* New York: Brunner/Mazel.

Colapinto, J. (1991). Structural family therapy. In A. M. Horne & J. L. Passmore (Eds.), *Family counseling and therapy.* Itasca, IL: F. E. Peacock.

Friesen, J. (1985). *Structural-strategic marriage and family therapy.* New York: Gardner Press.

Gurman, A. S., & Kniskern, D. P. (Eds.). (1981). *Handbook of family therapy.* New York: Brunner/Mazel.

Lane, M. (1970). *Introduction to structuralism.* New York: Basic Books.

Minuchin, S. (1974). *Families and family therapy.* Cambridge, MA: Harvard University Press.

Minuchin, S. (1981). Structural family therapy. In R. J. Green & J. L. Framo (Eds.), *Family therapy: Major contributions.* New York: International Universities Press.

Minuchin, S., & Fishman, C. H. (1981). *Family therapy techniques.* Cambridge, MA: Harvard University Press.

Minuchin, S., Montalvo, B., Guerney, B. G., Rosman, B. L., & Schumer, F. (1967). *Families of the slums.* New York: Basic Books.

Minuchin, S., & Nichols, M. P. (1993). *Family healing.* New York: Free Press.

Minuchin, S., Rosman, B., & Baker, L. (1978). *Psychosomatic families: Anorexia nervosa in context.* Cambridge, MA: Harvard University Press.

Nichols, M. P. (1984). *Family therapy, concepts and methods.* New York: Gardner Press.

Stanton, M. D., & Todd, T. C. (1979). Structural family therapy with drug addicts. In E. Kaufman & P. Kaufman (Eds.), *The family therapy of drug and alcohol abuse.* New York: Gardner Press.

Szapocznik, J., Murray, E., Scopetta, M., Hervis, O., Rio, A., Cohen, R., Rivas-Vazquez, A., & Posada, V. (1989). Structural family versus psychodynamic child therapy for problematic Hispanic boys. *Journal of Consulting and Clinical Psychology, 57,* 571–578.

Umbarger, C. (1983). *Structural family therapy.* New York: Grune and Stratton.

Walsh, W. (1980). *A primer of family therapy.* Springfield, IL: Charles C Thomas Press.

Strategic
Family Therapy

❖ **MAJOR THEORISTS:** Jay Haley and Cloe Madanes ❖

PRIMARY SOURCES FOR FURTHER READING

Strategies of Psychotherapy, Haley (1963)
*Uncommon Therapy: The Psychiatric Techniques of
    Milton H. Erickson, M.D.*, Haley (1973)
Leaving Home, Haley (1980)
Strategic Family Therapy, Madanes (1981)
*Behind the One-Way Mirror: Advances in the Practice of
    Strategic Therapy*, Madanes (1984)
Ordeal Therapy: Unusual Ways to Change Behavior,
    Haley (1984)
Problem-Solving Therapy, Haley (1987; 1st ed. 1971)
Sex, Love, and Violence: Strategies for Transformation,
    Madanes (1990)

Strategic family therapy is one of the major models of family therapy. However, it may be considered a second generation theory. Jay Haley describes this method as therapy where the therapist designs interventions that fit the problem. This chapter will focus on strategic family therapy as conceptualized and practiced by Jay Haley and Cloe Madanes. Readers are encouraged to review the works of other contributors to this model of family therapy as well.

Many variants of strategic family therapy have branched out from the core elements developed by Haley and Madanes. Additional names used to denote this general classification of family therapy include the Milan model, systemic therapy, brief therapy, and problem-solving therapy. These models have different emphases and nuances, yet they share a common origin and philosophical basis.

Jay Haley was born in 1923. His education included undergraduate work in library science at the University of California at Berkeley and graduate work in communication at Stanford. Following completion of his master's degree in 1953, Haley worked on the Project for the Study of Communication, which was directed by Gregory Bateson. Haley's involvement included the study of hypnosis, animal behavior, schizophrenia, families, and family therapy. Haley also entered private practice in psychotherapy during this time. Along with private practice, Haley has held professorships at the University of Pennsylvania, Howard University, and the University of Maryland. He worked at the Mental Research Institute and the Child Guidance Clinic as well as being the founder and co-director of the Family Therapy Institute of Washington, DC, with Cloe Madanes. A prolific writer, Haley has been involved with 13 books as author, co-author, or editor. He has also authored numerous journal articles on diverse topics.

Cloe Madanes states that her interest in psychology began when she was 14 years old. Her professional education in Argentina had a psychoanalytic orientation, and she was in analysis for five years. Exposure to a paper on double-bind theory by Bateson, Jackson, Haley, and Weakland (1956) piqued Madanes' interest in families and communication. In 1965, Madanes moved to Palo Alto and began studying family therapy at the Mental Research Institute. She also worked as a research assistant for

Paul Watzlawick. After three years, Madanes returned to Argentina where she accepted a position as a professor and clinical supervisor of family therapy. She came back to the United States in 1971 and worked at the Philadelphia Child Guidance Clinic with Minuchin, Haley, and Montalvo. Madanes subsequently left the Child Guidance Clinic and co-founded the Family Therapy Institute of Washington, DC, where she presently serves as co-director.

HISTORICAL INFLUENCES

Two influences figure prominently in the origin of strategic family therapy: Bateson's work on cybernetics, systems, and communication and Erickson's use of hypnosis and paradoxical directives in therapy. In conjunction with Don Jackson, John Weakland, and William Fry, Haley became involved with Bateson on research into communication. This diverse collection of individuals composed the initial membership of the now famous Palo Alto group. Their research on the families of individuals with schizophrenia spawned the "double-bind" concept, which was reported in the article "Toward a Theory of Schizophrenia" (Bateson, Jackson, Haley, & Weakland, 1956). This engendered an interest in the family treatment of schizophrenia.

Erickson's influence on strategic family therapy was felt when Haley and Weakland began weekend tutelage under Erickson at his home in Phoenix, Arizona. This initiated a long-standing collaboration between Erickson and Haley in which Haley studied and chronicled the clinical work of Erickson. The pragmatic, innovative, and sometimes incomprehensible work of Erickson is described in Haley's books *Strategies of Psychotherapy* (1963) and *Uncommon Therapy* (1973).

Haley's collaboration with Salvador Minuchin and Braulio Montalvo at the Philadelphia Child Guidance Clinic facilitated a sharing of ideas and the eventual convergence of strategic and structural family therapy models in numerous areas.

The strategic family therapy model continues to be refined by Arthur Bodin, Carlos Sluzki, Olga Silverstein, and Peggy Papp in their ongoing research and clinical practice.

PHILOSOPHY

The strategic family therapy model is based on the idea that families are rule-governed systems and can best be understood in this context. Furthermore, the presenting problem serves a function in the family that must be recognized. Symptoms are system maintained and system maintaining. And destructive ongoing cycles of interaction prevent the family or couple from achieving its basic purposes.

Developmental stages in the family life cycle are significant considerations, because halted development can lead to problems in later stages. In strategic family therapy the focus is on the present, and insight into the cause of the problem is less important than affecting a change in behavior or functioning.

THEORETICAL TENETS

The organization of a family is reflected in characteristic family behavioral patterns that are dependable and highly predictable. Within the family system there is also a hierarchy, a vertical organization usually related to the degree of influence one member has over another. In a conventional family hierarchical organization, family functioning is based on clear generational boundaries where the parents maintain control and authority. Alliances and coalitions, formations of within-family groups and other parts of the system that make the family a distinct entity, can alter the conventional hierarchy.

Two levels of communication must be attended to in strategic family therapy. Digital communication "consists of that class of messages where each statement has a specific referent and only that referent. Something happens or it does not happen; there is one stimulus and one response. . . . If A, and only if A, then Z and only Z" (Haley, 1987, p. 91). This type of communication is highly technical, formal, and content-oriented. Problems arise when digital communication is applied to human interactions because much of the message is lost. The second level of communication is analogic communication. Analogic communication has many referents and deals with the resemblances of one thing to another. It is highly nonverbal, informal, and contextual. In strategic family therapy, analogic communication is conveyed through a family's metaphors, body language, and symbolism. The understanding of analogic communication among individuals is crucial when conceptualizing and intervening through the relational context of the presenting problem.

The presenting problem is the concern or issue identified by the family that resulted in involvement in treatment. This becomes the focus of therapy and is "a type of behavior that is part of a sequence of acts between several people" (Haley, 1976, p. 2). This behavioral sequence serves to define the nature of the relationship and is frequently concerned with control issues. These behavioral sequences are termed symptoms, and symptoms may be viewed as gaining control of the relationship among family members. A frequently asked therapeutic question is, "What function does this symptom sense in the system?"

Power usually refers to the struggle to make rules in a family. In pathological family systems under stress, "the family attempts to rigidly hold to current rules and interactional structures rather than changing. The question of 'who makes the rules in this family?' becomes all important" (Thomas, 1992, p. 364).

The family life cycle, a process of development of the family that includes stages such as marriage, birth of first child, reduction in family size (e.g., children leaving home), and advanced age, is also a source of stress. Transitions between stages become focal points of assessment and treatment because the appearance of presenting problems frequently corresponds to the family encountering a developmental task.

FUNCTIONAL AND DYSFUNCTIONAL EFFECTS ON FAMILIES

Functional families have the characteristics of an open system. These characteristics include clear boundaries allowing adequate and predictable exchange of information within and without the family, adaptability, and organization. Haley notes that in most societies a functional family hierarchy has the parents at the top of the hierarchy in that they maintain the authority within the family. Functional families utilize effective communication processes that allow them to deal with the challenges posed by family developmental tasks and miscellaneous problems.

Three general types of problems are common in dysfunctional families (Haley, 1987). In dysfunctional families, problem solution is often at the wrong hierarchical level. These families typically deny the presence of a problem or create a problem where none exists. Dysfunctional families are characterized by unclear or inappropriate hierarchical structure. Haley notes that "if there is a fundamental rule of social organization, it is that an organization is in trouble when coalitions occur across levels of a hierarchy" (1976, p. 104). When such an interactional pattern becomes crystallized in a family, symptomatic behavior in one or more family members is highly likely.

In Madanes' work, the symptom is seen as representative of the underlying relational dynamic. An example of symptom as metaphor is an asthmatic child whose presenting concerns symbolize his or her mother's feeling of being "suffocated" in her relationship with her husband. Haley (1973) notes that presenting problems frequently arise when the family encounters a developmental task in its life cycle. Symptoms are likely to occur at points of transition between stages. Some families develop problems because they are not able to make the necessary transition from one stage to the next stage. When there is a disruption or failure to move to the next stage in the family life cycle, dysfunction occurs. The failure or disruption is because the family is having difficulty mastering the tasks inherent in that stage of the life cycle. In short, the problem is not the identified patient but the way the family reacts and attempts to adapt to the next stage it is approaching or has entered.

ASSESSMENT AND DIAGNOSIS

Assessment in strategic family therapy involves an ongoing process of observation of the relational dynamics of the family. Particularly, therapeutic attention is focused on family patterns, coalitions, alliances, communication (e.g., analogic, digital), and power.

Diagnoses are framed as interactional sequences among family members that pose problems and prevent successful adaptation. Diagnostic labels that suggest pathology in one family member are avoided.

Assessment begins with the first contact with the family as the therapist begins to form initial hypotheses about family dynamics. These hypotheses are tested through ongoing observation of the family, and revisions to the hypotheses are made as needed. Frequently, diagnosis is initiated by making an intervention and then observing how the family system responds. The focus is on specific problems and the therapeutic strategies that can interrupt the patterns maintaining the problem.

GOALS OF TREATMENT

A hallmark of strategic family therapy is addressing the presenting problem as identified by the family. This is cogently stated by Haley (1987):

> The first obligation of a therapist is to change the presenting problem offered. If that is not accomplished, the therapy is a failure. Therapists should not let themselves be distracted into other matters so that they forget this primary goal. Moreover, by focusing on the symptoms the therapist gains the most leverage and has the most opportunity for bringing about change. (p. 135)

The Mental Research Institute (MRI) style of strategic family therapy has a goal of only changing the presenting problem. Haley has a more inclusive aim in that he also strives to alter the relational dynamics associated with the behavior. It is not a goal of strategic family therapy to work toward family insight regarding the interactional processes.

TREATMENT PROCESS

The treatment process in strategic family therapy is pragmatic, brief, and orchestrated by the therapist. The objective of the treatment process is to interrupt behavioral sequences to promote goal attainment.

Change occurs when the therapist actively intervenes to alter the family's typical interactional patterns:

> When dealing with a governed, homeostatic system that is maintained by repeating sequences of behavior, the therapist changes those sequences by shifting the ways people respond to each other because of the ways they must respond to the therapist. (Haley, 1987, p. 186)

Five basic stages can be used to describe this process. The first stage involves establishing a therapeutic relationship. Establishing a trusting relationship between the family and the therapist is a crucial component of promoting change. The therapist joins the family system by greeting and interacting with each family member. Typically the parents will be engaged first, then they will be asked to introduce their children. This serves the purpose of allowing the therapist to observe the hierarchical structure within the family. The therapist begins to form tentative hypotheses about the family dynamics based on observations of the family (e.g., who sits by whom and who interrupts and when).

The second stage of this process involves clarifying the presenting problem. The objective is to form a clear understanding of who is involved in problem maintenance and how this occurs. Each family member is asked to describe the problem. The strategy the therapist chooses regarding how and when to procure this information is very important and may differ given the particulars of the family. For example, by addressing the least involved child first, the therapist demonstrates the importance of each member of the family (Haley, 1987). It is important to specify the problem very clearly and specifically (i.e., in observable and measurable terms) so the family will know when they are successful.

The third stage is the interaction stage. Interaction among family members is observed by the therapist so system functioning can be assessed. The therapist may encourage a child to engage in the problematic behavior in the session to observe the family dynamics with regard to areas of dysfunction such as diffuse boundaries, coalitions, and triangles.

Stage four is setting goals. The therapist assists the family in describing what life will be like at the end of treatment. A slightly different perspective or summary of the family's goal may be presented by the therapist to begin to reframe the presenting problem. Ultimately, the specific goals may be formalized through the use of a verbal or written contract.

The fifth and final stage is to develop a plan. A plan is formulated that takes into account the dysfunctional family hierarchy and the family's stage in the life cycle. The therapist has the final determination as to how to achieve the goals. The therapist may employ intervention as a therapeutic tool, using directives to create new behaviors. These directives may be rehearsed in the session but need to be carried out in real life. Interventions may not lead directly to the family goal; rather, intermediate steps may be involved as described by Hoffman (1981):

> Haley thinks of therapy in terms of a step-by-step change in the way the family is organized, so that it goes from one type of abnormal organization to another type before a more normal organization is finally achieved. By then, presumably, the symptom is no longer necessary. (p. 280)

Generally, the therapeutic process involves meeting with the entire family for weekly sessions. The duration in therapy is brief (i.e., customarily between six and ten sessions). Toward the end of treatment, sessions may be extended over longer periods of time (e.g., one to two sessions per month). A posttreatment follow-up session may also be a component of the treatment process.

TECHNIQUES

The use of directives to initiate or maintain change is the cornerstone of strategic family therapy. Directives serve three basic functions in therapy:

❖ to promote behavior change and new subjective experiences for family members,

❖ to intensify the therapist-client relationship through the use of tasks, and

❖ to gather useful information about the family by noting the family's response to the directives.

In general, the family can manifest three types of responses: successfully complete the directive, partially complete the directive, or resist the directive. The nature of the family response to a directive will have an impact on later directives. For example, the therapist may choose to employ a paradoxical directive if the family has previously resisted straightforward directives. Pragmatic in nature, the strategic family therapy model allows for limitless creativity in designing and implementing directives that will address a family's unique concerns.

General types of techniques can be modified to fit each unique family. Straightforward directives are tasks designed to change the interactional sequence in the family. They can include advice, explanations, or suggestions. Straightforward directives are presented with the expectation that the family will not resist the task. Madanes (1981) states that straightforward directives are planned with the goal of changing sequences of interaction in the family. The interventions may be employed to involve previously disengaged family members, promote agreement and good feeling, increase positive interchanges, provide information, and help a family organize in more functional ways. This process may involve setting rules, defining generational boundaries, and establishing individual goals and plans to achieve those goals. Haley (1976) provides many suggestions for increasing the family's cooperation with the directives that are presented, including: be precise, get everyone in the family to do something, start with small tasks in the session that the family can continue at home, anticipate what may go wrong, and structure a task that fits with the performance level of the family.

Paradoxical directives involve tasks in which success is based on the family defying the instructions or following them to an extreme point and ultimately recoiling, producing change. Typically these directives are presented when the therapist has reason to believe the family will resist a straightforward directive. In presenting a paradoxical directive, Haley describes eight steps:

1. Establish a trusting relationship with the family where change is anticipated.

2. Define the problem in clear, observable terms.
3. Set specific, behavioral goals.
4. Design a plan that is delivered in a precise and authoritative manner.
5. Disqualify the current authority on the problem.
6. Deliver the paradoxical directive in a sincere manner.
7. Encourage symptomatic behavior.
8. Avoid taking credit for family change or expressing confusion over the improvement.

Reframing, also referred to as relabeling, positive interpretation, positive connotation, or reattribution, is an intervention in which the therapist offers a different (typically nonblaming and positive) view of the presenting problem that enables the family members to think and behave differently within the new context.

Prescribing the symptom is a type of paradoxical intervention in which the client is directed to perform the symptomatic behavior. If followed, it demonstrates that the symptom is under voluntary control; if resisted, the client has demonstrated that he or she can give up the symptom.

Pretend techniques are paradoxical interventions in which clients are directed to "pretend" to have a symptom. Paradoxically, since the behavior was the result of pretending, the symptom may be reclassified as voluntary and unreal and thus able to be altered (Goldenberg & Goldenberg, 1991). Madanes (1981) has developed pretend techniques that utilize humor and fantasy, which serve to decrease defiance and resistance.

Restraining changes are paradoxical interventions in which the therapist attempts to discourage the family from moving too fast or even denies the possibility of change. And ordeals are paradoxical interventions in which the family is given a task that makes it more difficult for the family to have the symptom than to give it up.

Metaphorical tasks are directives that involve activities or conversations that symbolically relate to the presenting problem and thereby indirectly facilitate change. A well-known example involves having a couple with sexual difficulties describe their preferences for the consumption of an evening meal (which symbolically represents the consummation of a sexual interlude).

A devil's pact is a task to which the family must commit before the therapist discloses it. The family is advised that the task is extremely demanding, and therefore they must decide whether or not they really want to resolve the presenting issue.

Using empowerment, the therapist may inform the family that they must be doing something right or the problem would be worse. The family's sense of failure is explained as a result of their trying too hard. This serves to bolster family morale and their expectation for change.

An observing therapy team watching the session through a one-way mirror can be used to influence the treatment process as well as to supervise and train family therapists. Peggy Papp (1983) has developed a variant of this approach that she calls the Greek Chorus in which observers behind the mirror send messages to the family regarding the process in the session and the dilemma of change.

ROLE OF THE THERAPIST

In strategic family therapy, the therapist is directive, tactical, warm, and able to negotiate the terms of therapy such that therapy remains problem focused and in control. Friesen (1985) suggests that the role of the strategic therapist is similar to that of the structural therapist in that:

1. The therapist is an active agent who joins the family in a personal relationship in order to make structural and interactional changes in the family.

2. The therapist must become a real member of the family and be accepted and trusted as an empathic, approachable helper.

3. The therapist needs some distance from the family to ensure objectivity and autonomy.

4. The therapist needs to provide a supportive but challenging therapeutic relationship.

5. The therapist must be capable of intense relating, rapid assessing, and active intervening. This requires the ability to develop a flexible, creative, unpredictable, and engaging therapeutic style.

6. The therapist requires a repertoire of techniques and a knowledge of timing. He or she needs to know how to adjust intensity and to regulate pressure and involvement.

7. The therapist must learn to use self as the most important instrument of intervention.

8. Resistance is resolved through the relationship, including use of personal charisma, knowledge, influence, and strength. (p. 13)

Haley (1987) stresses the importance of the therapist assuming a neutral stance when working with the family system:

> At the most general level, therapists should not side consistently with anyone in the family against anyone else. But that does not mean they should not temporarily side with one against another, because that is in fact the only way therapists can induce change. If they only place their "weight" in coalitions equally, they will continue the sequence as it was. In the same way, if they only join one person against another, they may maintain the system as it was by simply becoming part of the deadlocked struggle. That task is more complex: the therapist must temporarily join in different coalitions while ultimately not siding with anyone against anyone. (p. 126)

EVALUATION OF THE STRATEGIC FAMILY THERAPY MODEL

Much of the supporting evidence for the efficacy of strategic family therapy is anecdotal. However, there is empirical research to support the effectiveness of strategic family therapy. Brown and Christensen (1986) note that research in strategic family therapy has demonstrated more scientific vigor when compared to other models. Gurman and Kniskern (1981) provide an extensive list of studies that describe the different presenting problems to which strategic family therapy has been applied including schizophrenia, anxiety, depression, delinquency, behavior problems, tinnitus, stomach aches, and work problems.

Although support regarding the efficacy of strategic family therapy has been mixed (Schilson, 1991), numerous studies do provide positive findings. A study involving the treatment of delinquents by Alexander and Parsons (1973) compared strategic-oriented family therapy with a client-centered family approach, an eclectic-dynamic family approach, and a no-treatment control group. The strategic model had markedly superior results compared to the other conditions in that recidivism was cut in half. The remaining treatment conditions did not result in significant differences in treatment outcome. A three-year follow-up study showed that problems for siblings of the subjects receiving the strategic treatment were significantly lower compared to the siblings of subjects receiving the different treatment conditions. A study by Langsley, Machotka, and Flomenhaft (1971) compared out-patient strategic-like family treatment (i.e., family crisis therapy) with psychiatric hospitalization. Improved cost-effectiveness of the strategic approach was demonstrated by an 18-month follow-up evaluation that showed the hospitalization group had over twice the number of hospital days (subsequent to the hospital days that were part of the hospitalization treatment process) and six times the treatment cost. A short-term follow-up study on families that received strategic treatment through the Mental Research Institute for a variety of presenting concerns showed that 40% were successful and 32% were seen as significantly improved (Weakland, Fisch, Watzlawick, & Bodin, 1974).

In a review of the research on strategic family therapy, Gurman and Kniskern (1981) note:

> A strategic orientation to family therapy either shows (a) substantially better results, or (b) considerable promise, when compared with several other (standard) forms of treatment. This is especially true when issues of cost efficiency are considered. (p. 396)

Nichols and Schwartz (1991) provide the caveat that generalization of research results on strategic family therapy should be done cautiously because empirically rigorous studies are few in number and because strategic family therapy is not a homogeneous approach (i.e., the specific types of treatment strategies utilized in the studies can vary considerably).

Schilson (1991) describes the primary challenge inherent in performing sound empirical research on strategic family therapy as the difficulty of making research design requirements compatible with the scope and function of the therapy process. She adds that more research needs to be conducted on this model, particularly regarding the critical components of treatment and the long-term effects.

REFERENCES

Alexander, J., & Parsons, B. (1973). Short-term behavioral intervention with delinquent families: Impact on family process and recidivism. *Journal of Abnormal Psychology, 81,* 219–225.

Bateson, G., Jackson, D., Haley, J., & Weakland, J. (1956). Toward a theory of schizophrenia. *Behavioral Science, 1,* 251–264.

Brown, J. H., & Christensen, D. H. (1986). *Family therapy: Theory and practice.* Pacific Grove, CA: Brooks/Cole.

Friesen, J. (1985). *Structural-strategic marriage and family therapy.* New York: Gardner Press.

Goldenberg, I., & Goldenberg, H. (1991). *Family therapy: An overview.* Pacific Grove, CA: Brooks/Cole.

Gurman, A. S., & Kniskern, D. P. (Eds.). (1981). *Handbook of family therapy.* New York: Brunner/Mazel.

Haley, J. (1963). *Strategies of psychotherapy.* New York: Grune & Stratton.

Haley, J. (1973). *Uncommon therapy: The psychiatric techniques of Milton H. Erickson, M.D.* New York: W. W. Norton.

Haley, J. (1976). *Problem-solving therapy.* San Francisco: Jossey-Bass.

Haley, J. (1980). *Leaving home: The therapy of disturbed young people.* New York: McGraw-Hill.

Haley, J. (1984). *Ordeal therapy: Unusual ways to change behavior.* San Francisco: Jossey-Bass.

Haley, J. (1987). *Problem-solving therapy* (2nd ed.). San Francisco: Jossey-Bass.

Hoffman, L. (1981). *Foundation of family therapy.* New York: Basic Books.

Langsley, D., Machotka, P., & Flomenhaft, K. (1971). Avoiding mental hospital admission: A follow-up study. *American Journal of Psychiatry, 127,* 1391–1394.

Madanes, C. (1981). *Strategic family therapy.* San Francisco: Jossey-Bass.

Madanes, C. (1984). *Behind the one-way mirror: Advances in the practice of strategic therapy.* San Francisco: Jossey-Bass.

Madanes, C. (1990). *Sex, love, and violence: Strategies for transformation.* New York: W. W. Norton.

Nichols, M. P., & Schwartz, R. C. (1991). *Family therapy: Concepts and methods* (2nd ed.). Boston: Allyn and Bacon.

Papp, P. (1983). *The process of change.* New York: Guilford.

Schilson, E. A. (1991). Strategic therapy. In A. M. Horne & J. L. Passmore (Eds.), *Family counseling and therapy.* Itasca, IL: F. E. Peacock.

Thomas, M. B. (1992). *An introduction to marital and family therapy.* New York: Merrill.

Weakland, J., Fisch, R., Watzlawick, P., & Bodin, A. (1974). Brief therapy: Focused problem resolution. *Family Process, 13,* 141–168.

Milan Model of
Family Systems Therapy

**MAJOR THEORISTS: Mara Selvini-Palazzoli,
Luigi Boscolo, Gianfranco Cecchin,
and Giuliana Prata**

PRIMARY SOURCES FOR FURTHER READING

*Self Starvation: From the Intrapsychic to the Trans-
personal Approach to Anorexia Nervosa,* Selvini-
Palazzoli (1978)
*Paradox and Counterparadox: A New Model in the
Therapy of the Family in Schizophrenic Transaction,*
Selvini-Palazzoli, Boscolo, Cecchin, & Prata (1978)
*Milan Systemic Family Therapy: Conversations in Theory
and Practice,* Boscolo, Cecchin, Hoffman, & Penn
(1987)
*Family Games: General Models of Psychotic Processes in
the Family,* Selvini-Palazzoli, Cirillo, Selvini, &
Sorrention (1989)

Typically classified as a type of communication or strategic model along with the Mental Research Institute communication or interactional model and the strategic family therapy model of Haley and Madanes, the Milan model is also referred to as systemic family therapy, strategic family therapy, and long-brief family therapy (i.e., "long" in that the time between sessions and total duration in therapy are long; "brief" in that the number of sessions is few). Of the varieties of strategic or communication models, the Milan systemic family therapy model remains truest to Gregory Bateson's systemic concepts and methods. There is a focus on process (interactional sequences) over structure and more emphasis on the past and the history of family patterns.

Mara Selvini-Palazzoli was a psychiatrist trained in the psychoanalytic treatment of children. In 1967 she founded the Center for Family Studies, which was designed to address the need for community family therapy as a result of deinstitutionalization of patients in Italy. By 1971, the Milan associates, comprised of psychiatrists including Selvini-Palazzoli, Boscolo, Cecchin, and Prata, had adopted a systemic approach to family research inspired by the work of Gregory Bateson and Jay Haley. Currently two major camps exist in Milan systemic family therapy: The Nuovo Centro Team (including Selvini-Palazzoli and Prata) emphasizes family systems research and the Centro Team (including Boscolo and Cecchin) emphasizes training.

HISTORICAL INFLUENCES

Members of the original Milan team were psychoanalytically trained psychiatrists who became frustrated with the minimal results they obtained when using long-term psychoanalytic therapy with severely disturbed patients (e.g., patients with diagnoses of schizophrenia or an eating disorder). In 1971 the Milan team adopted a systemic orientation with the ecosystemic work of Gregory Bateson serving as a conceptual foundation. The team was also influenced by the strategic therapy of Jay Haley and for a period of time had Paul Watzlawick serve as a consultant to the group. Ultimately, the Milan team isolated themselves to form a new therapeutic model.

The work of cognitive biologists (e.g., Maturana and von Foerster) and constructivists (e.g., von Glasersfeld) has been described as having an impact on the Milan model (Boscolo, Cecchin, Hoffman, & Penn, 1987). In the U.S., the Milan model has been influential in the work of members of the Acherman Institute for Family Therapy including Peggy Penn, Joel Bergman, and Lynn Hoffman. The Milan model has developed through time and continues to evolve through ongoing theorizing, research, practice, and training.

PHILOSOPHY

The Milan model has a systemic epistemology grounded in the work of Gregory Bateson (see Chapter 1 for basic systemic concepts). In this model the most complex explains the simplest (i.e., there is a movement from linear hypotheses to circular, triadic hypotheses to account for behavior). The therapists (including the observing or consulting team) and the family make up a therapy system; thus the barrier between the family system and the therapist is removed. This concept is related to the systemic assumption that client-therapist objectivity is invalid. The presenting problem is recognized as serving a function in the family system.

Patterns of interaction can be passed down through generations, and therefore the history of the family is important. The Centro Team focuses less on the homeostatic process in systems and more on the view that the change process in families is primary. Relatively long time periods between sessions are necessary to allow systemic interventions to incubate and have maximal effect.

Cognitive processes (i.e., ideas, beliefs, perceptions, fantasies) are addressed along with behaviors:

> From the beginning the Milan group took mental artifacts as seriously as behaviors. Their philosophy of change was tied to the notion that families come in with "maps" of what is going on and that the therapist attempts to challenge or shift these "maps." (Boscolo et al., 1987, p. 19)

THEORETICAL TENETS

Neutrality is the basic therapeutic stance, and it arises out of Bateson's concept of cybernetic circularity. Given this approach, the therapy team does not get caught in family coalitions or alliances. Rather than being "nonpositional," the team is "multipositional" (Boscolo et al., 1987). Imbroglio is a dyadic phenomenon in which a parent bestows special favors on one offspring as a means of acting out issues against his or her spouse.

Family games are seen as an interactive organization in the family that has evolved over time. All families have games, but not all games are pathological. A symptom in a family member can be an indicator that someone in the family system is negatively affected by the family game. Counter games, a generic label for a therapeutic prescription designed to substitute new rules in the family game, alter both the elements of the game and the family structure (Stanton, 1981).

Using Bateson's (1972) definition of information as "a difference that makes a difference," the Milan model searches for differences in behavior, perception, and relationships among family members that uncover family connections that perpetuate dysfunction. Alliances, a type of relationship that can occur among family members, sometimes involve the members of the alliance in opposition to other family members. An alliance between a child and a parent against the other parent can be part of the pathological family game. A strong alliance between parents is part of healthy family functioning and may be a treatment goal.

The Centro Team supplants the term *family system* with the more inclusive term *significant system,* which includes those units (i.e., persons or institutions) involved in the attempt to alleviate the presenting problem. The significant system usually includes the treatment center, the family, and the referral source, and may include other systems such as schools or the court.

Cybernetic circularity, a Batesonian concept that describes the recursive and interconnected nature of living systems (Bateson, 1972), served as the theoretical foundation for the following concepts and practices in the Milan model of systemic family therapy: neutrality, circular questioning, and hypothesizing (Boscolo et al., 1987, p. 10).

FUNCTIONAL AND DYSFUNCTIONAL EFFECTS ON FAMILIES

Patterns of interaction in a family system can become fixed and predictable. Patterns that are dysfunctional can be perpetuated across situations and generations of a family. Dysfunctional families make "epistemological errors" in that they follow an outdated "map" or view of reality as a guide to appropriate behavior. The games in dysfunctional families are covert.

There is minimal focus on the functioning of healthy families, although it is possible to speculate on the characteristics of a functional family by generating characteristics opposite those of a dysfunctional family. For example, a healthy family would not make significant epistemological errors and would follow a basically accurate "map."

ASSESSMENT AND DIAGNOSIS

Assessment of family problems is conceptualized within a relational context, and symptoms are viewed as indicative of problems in the family system. The therapy team works to maintain a systemic mind-set when conceptualizing family dynamics through the conscious use of accurate languaging. This entails trying to decrease verbal descriptions connoting a linear view (e.g., "the daughter is angry") and replacing them with a circular view that places the behavior within the family context (e.g., "the daughter is angering").

Bateson's concept of cybernetic circularity is transformed into an assessment process in the form of hypothesizing (Boscolo et al., 1987). The therapy team, in conjunction with the family, formulates hypotheses about the nature of the family's problem. These hypotheses are subjected to ongoing evaluation and revision as more information about the family is amassed. The hypotheses are not judged in terms of being right or wrong; rather, they are evaluated in terms of their usefulness in leading to new information that helps the family move. Information is derived from the family by observing interactions, by their response to prescriptions, and by asking questions. Questions asked address specific issues in the context of the family system (e.g., Why is help being sought? Who most enjoys to fight? What is the motivation for change?).

The treatment team uses a balancing formula to assess the likelihood of success in therapy. If more weight is given to the side that favors change, work continues with the family. If the balance is in favor of maintaining the family game, the family is informed that therapy is not currently indicated or referrals are provided. Even though assessment is an ongoing process throughout the treatment period, sessions one through three are more intentionally diagnostic in nature, while session four (and any subsequent session) has more emphasis on treatment.

The Nuovo Centro Team has identified and labeled commonly observed patterns of dysfunction such as dirty games and psychotic games (Selvini-Palazzoli et al., 1989).

GOALS OF TREATMENT

An overriding goal for the therapy team is to have the family discover, interrupt, and eventually change the rules of their game (i.e., the relational dynamic underlying the family dysfunction). The family may create a solution to their problem that is different from the therapists' goal. The parental couple is encouraged to regain the skills that will enhance their leadership function.

The Nuovo Centro Team desires not only symptom alleviation and change in interpersonal processes but also wants the family to understand the meaning of the symptoms (i.e., the connection between the symptom and the family game). An additional goal is to interrupt the rigid game and force the family to create more flexible ways to relate.

TREATMENT PROCESS

A hallmark of the Milan systemic family therapy treatment process is the extended time between sessions, typically one month (to allow prescriptions to have full impact on the family system).

The number of sessions averages between 5 and 8, with 12 sessions being near the upper limit.

The preparation process typically follows a standard format. First, a telephone interview is conducted in which one team member collects pertinent information from the referring family member (e.g., the nature of the problem and its history, general information about the nuclear and extended family). Typically, the telephone interview is used just once prior to the initial session. Then a pre-session meeting is held in which therapy team members meet to review the information collected in the telephone interview. Initial hypotheses are formulated to help the team understand the family and plan interviewing strategies.

The first treatment session is a family session. The therapists have their first direct contact with the family. The logistics of the therapy sessions (e.g., the observing therapy team and the use of videotape) are described to the family. The therapy team is split into two subgroups: the therapists (initially female and male co-therapists were the norm; currently a solitary therapist may have direct contact with the family) and the observing team. The therapists interview the family while the observing team observes the process of treatment. Both therapy subgroups focus on interpersonal information from the family that will illuminate the family game. The information that is gathered is examined within the context of the working hypotheses that were previously developed. After the working hypotheses have been investigated sufficiently, a structured break occurs in the session.

During the break, the therapy subgroups reunite to evaluate and refine the initial hypothesis or the hypotheses that have emerged from the session. From the new systemic information that has emerged from the session, a positive connotation and prescription are developed that will help the family members see the interconnectedness of presenting issues from different perspectives. Following the break, the therapy subgroup presents the positive connotation message to the family regarding the presenting problem. This is called communicating the prescription. A prescription or homework task for the family may then be presented dependent upon the particular concerns of the family and the stage of the treatment process. The prescription, if used, is delivered in a concise, simple, and understandable manner. Other interventions may be utilized at this stage of therapy as well (e.g., split-team intervention and invariant prescriptions).

Typically, the first session involves meeting with parents, children, extended family, and other potential participants who may be involved in the family game (e.g., other professionals, neighbors, friends, baby-sitters, and so forth). The first session may be the only opportunity for the team to get information about the broad social context in which the family operates.

From the first contact with the family through the third session, the emphasis is on assessment even though the family is discouraged from directly discussing the presenting symptom. Although continued assessment occurs in subsequent meetings, session four and later sessions have a greater emphasis on change processes.

In the second session, only nuclear family members are invited to return. In this meeting, changes in the family are recognized, and increased assessment on more personal matters is accomplished (i.e., on issues not appropriate to expose to individuals outside the nuclear family). Even less time is spent talking about the presenting problem. The second interview has three components:

❖ *Connecting phase:* Therapists continue to collect information from the family, and the family is taught to observe and recognize differences.

❖ *Analysis phase:* Focus is placed upon interactions within the nucleus of the family network.

❖ *Testing phase:* Therapists test the motivation of the family and explore parts of the system that will support a discontinuation of the game.

Only the parents attend the third session. They are asked questions related to issues handed down from their respective families of origin, their marriage, and their parenting functions. At the conclusion of the third session, if the team continues to view the parents as motivated to change, the couple will be given a secret prescription, a set of behaviors to use in the home. The parents keep a diary of the responses to the prescribed behaviors and bring that record to the next session.

The fourth through final sessions have a focus on two primary issues: reviewing each parent's observations regarding the secret prescription (e.g., how did the children react, how have things changed at home) and additional prescriptions provided by the therapy team.

TECHNIQUES

Circular questioning is an interviewing technique developed out of Bateson's concept of cybernetic circularity. Particularly during the assessment phase of treatment (sessions one through three), circular questions are used to expose the family dynamics and enable the therapy team to develop, test, and refine provisional hypotheses. The process of questioning from the therapists also engenders a process in the family wherein they begin to question their own processes in a different way, which makes solution generation possible. Questions relevant to the present issue, relationships in the family, and differences in family members' perceptions are posed. Basically, circular questions ask one member to comment on or speculate about other family members' beliefs, feelings, and behavior. Examples of circular questions are:

❖ If your sister were to get married, who would miss her the most?

❖ If I ask your father, will he agree with your sister or your mother?

❖ John, what do you think has kept your mother from hearing your complaints?

(Horne & Passmore, 1991, p. 244)

Hypothesizing, a process wherein the therapy team speculates (in advance of the family session) what may be responsible for maintaining the family's problems, is central to the Milan model. Unless the therapists come prepared to the session with hypotheses to be tested, there is a risk that the family may impose its faulty problem definition and therein prevent solutions. Hypothesizing by the therapy team continues throughout the family's tenure in therapy.

The use of positive connotation, positive motives attributed to an individual's or family's symptomatic behavior patterns, is critical to success in the Milan model. Different terms used to describe a similar process in other models include reframing, noble ascription, and positive attribution. In the Milan model, positive connotation denotes not only a technique but, more important, an attitude shift for the therapists toward a more systemic orientation.

Prescriptions are a paradoxical intervention in which the family or certain members of the family are directed to perform the symptomatic behavior. If the prescription is followed, it demonstrates that the symptom is under voluntary control; if the directive is resisted, it is done so by the family giving up the symptom. Unlike Haley's use of prescriptions, the Milan model does not use prescriptions to arouse defiance and resistance. MacKinnon (1983) notes that by not trying to provoke resistance to change, the Milan model enables the family to discover its own solutions.

A split team intervention is a type of prescription in which the family receives a message that the therapy team has different opinions or ideas regarding a particular family dynamic. Hearing both sides of the issue allows the family game to be uncovered, gives the therapists in the session leverage (e.g., we tend to believe the family's explanation), and allows the family to find their own resolution. An example of a split-team intervention would be to tell (or write a letter to) the family: "Half the therapy team sees father as showing his caring for the family when he protects daughter from mother; the other half of the team views father's behavior as a way to help mother deal with a daughter who is quite powerful."

Ritual and ceremony are methods of prescription where family members put into action a series of behaviors designed to alter the family game. The therapists spell out the specifics of the prescription in minute detail (i.e., who does what, where, when, how). Here is a specific text for a ritual delivered to a family (Selvini-Palazzoli et al., 1978):

> On even days of the week—Tuesdays, Thursdays, and Saturdays—beginning from tomorrow onwards until the date of the next session and fixing the time between ___ o'clock and ___ o'clock (making sure that the whole family will be at home during

this time) whatever Z does (name of patient, followed by a list of his symptomatic behavior) father will decide alone, at his absolute discretion, what to do with Z. Mother will have to behave as if she were not there. On odd days of the week—Mondays, Wednesdays, and Fridays—at the same time, whatever Z may do, mother will have full power to decide what course of action to follow regarding Z. Father will have to behave as if he were not there. On Sundays everyone must behave spontaneously. Each parent, on the days assigned to him or her, must record in a diary any infringement by the partner of the prescription according to which he is expected to behave as if he were not there. (In some cases the job of recording the possible mistakes of one of the parents has been entrusted to a child acting as a recorder or to the patient himself, if he is fit for the task.) (p. 5)

An invariant prescription is a specific type of prescription Selvini-Palazzoli uses with families that have schizophrenic or anorexic children. This intervention is based on the assumption that a common family game is occurring in these families where the symptomatic child attempts to take sides in a stalemated relationship between the parents (Simon, 1987). Following an initial family interview, the therapists see the parents separately and give them a fixed sequence of directives designed to promote clear and stable boundaries between the generations; the invariant prescription reads as follows (Selvini-Palazzoli, 1986):

Keep everything about this session absolutely secret at home. Every now and then, start going out in the evenings before dinner. Nobody must be forewarned. Just leave a written note saying, "We'll not be home tonight." If, when you come back, one of your (daughters) inquires where you have been, just answer calmly, "These things concern only the two of us." Moreover, each of you will keep a notebook, carefully hidden and out of the children's reach. In these notebooks each of you, separately, will register the date and describe the verbal and nonverbal behavior of each child, or other family members, which seemed to be connected with the records because it's extremely important that nothing be forgotten or omitted. Next time you will again come alone, with your notebooks, and read aloud what has happened in the meantime. (pp. 341–342)

Disappearances are a component of the invariant prescription in which the parents "disappear" from the household and provide the children with minimal information regarding their actions and whereabouts. This technique serves to uncover and alter the family game.

Parents as therapists is a technique or therapeutic process typically used in the fourth session, after the parents have proven their commitment to secrecy from the children. The therapists appoint the parents as co-therapists and consequently "have the pathogenic couple transform into one that can 'cure' their child and, in the process, 'cure' themselves by modifying their relational pattern" (Selvini-Palazzoli et al., 1989, p. 236).

Counterparadox is a technique used to instill a therapeutic double bind in the family system to undo a pre-existing family double-bind message. For example, a common counterparadox is to inform the family that even though the therapists are change agents, they do not want to alter what seems to be a workable homeostatic balance in the family, and consequently prescribe "no change" for now (Selvini-Palazzoli et al., 1978).

Instigation is a phenomenon in which a family member pits someone else against a third party as part of an ongoing interactional process.

ROLE OF THE THERAPIST

The role of the therapists in the therapeutic process occurs on three levels (Selvini-Palazzoli et al., 1989). In Level 1, the therapists avoid getting entangled in the family game and thereby fail to further its dysfunctional, repetitive pattern. In Level 2, the therapists use prescriptions to invite the family to start playing a different game. And in Level 3, the therapists unmask the game.

The therapists must remain in control of the therapy process, yet they tend to limit their expert opinion position when using the Milan model. Forming a working alliance with the parents of the nuclear family is a critical function of therapy. Therapists obtain information from the nuclear family and from members of the extended system in a way that is focused yet nonconfrontational. Reactions to questions are noted, and information from questions is integrated into existing notions of family dynamics. Earlier formulations of the Milan systemic family therapy model had the therapy team in a more confrontational position relative to the family system. Currently, a more collaborative stance is espoused by the Nuovo Centro Team (Selvini-Palazzoli et al., 1989):

> A collaborative atmosphere will enhance the family's willingness to listen, which in turn allows the therapist to listen not only with the head but also with the heart. It also lets the therapist feel free to ask the family members for help in understanding their dilemma. When family members see the therapist as someone who has joined them in seeking a solution to their problem, and has abandoned all reticence in doing so, the all-round emotional atmosphere will undergo a momentous change for the better. (p. 250)

EVALUATION OF THE MILAN SYSTEMIC FAMILY THERAPY MODEL

The Milan model has been applied to a diversity of presenting concerns, although two types of presenting issues have received particular attention: families with a member with schizophrenia and those with a member with an eating disorder.

A strength of the Milan model is that its application is more consistent with its theory relative to other strategic models (Goldenberg & Goldenberg, 1991). Similar to other strategic models, much of the supporting evidence is anecdotal (refer to the evaluation of strategic family therapy for an overview of the empirical research on this related model). The Milan model is particularly difficult to evaluate using standard empirical processes because of the extended time between sessions.

REFERENCES

Bateson, G. (1972). *Steps to an ecology of mind.* New York: E. P. Dutton.

Boscolo, L., Cecchin, G., Hoffman, L., & Penn, P. (1987). *Milan systemic family therapy: Conversations in theory and practice.* New York: Basic Books.

Goldenberg, I., & Goldenberg, H. (1991). *Family therapy: An overview.* Pacific Grove, CA: Brooks/Cole.

Horne, A. M., & Passmore, L. J. (1991). *Family counseling and therapy.* Itasca, IL: F. E. Peacock.

MacKinnon, L. (1983). Contrasting strategic and Milan therapies. *Family Process, 22,* 425–440.

Selvini-Palazzoli, M. (1978). *Self starvation: From the intrapsychic to the transpersonal approach to anorexia nervosa.* New York: Aronson.

Selvini-Palazzoli, M. (1986). Towards a general model of psychotic family games. *Journal of Marital and Family Therapy, 12,* 339–349.

Selvini-Palazzoli, M., Boscolo, L., Cecchin, G. F., & Prata, G. (1978). *Paradox and counterparadox: A new model in the therapy of the family in schizophrenic transaction.* New York: Aronson.

Selvini-Palazzoli, M., Cirillo, S., Selvini, M., & Sorrention, A. M. (1989). *Family games: General models of psychotic processes in the family.* New York: W. W. Norton.

Simon, R. (1987). Goodbye paradox, hello invariant prescription: An interview with Mara Selvini-Palazzoli. *The Family Therapy Networker, 11* (5), 16–33.

Stanton, M. D. (1981). Strategic approaches to family therapy. In A. S. Gurman & D. P. Kniskern (Eds.), *Handbook of family therapy.* New York: Brunner/Mazel.

Solution-Focused Brief Family Therapy

❖ **MAJOR THEORIST: Steve de Shazer** ❖

PRIMARY SOURCES FOR FURTHER READING

Patterns of Brief Family Therapy: An Ecosystemic Approach, de Shazer (1982)
Keys to Solutions in Brief Therapy, de Shazer (1985)
Clues: Investigating Solutions in Brief Therapy, de Shazer (1988)
A Guide to Practice: Constructing Solutions in In-Home Treatment, Berg (1990)
Putting Differences to Work, de Shazer (1991)
Working with the Problem Drinker, Berg & Miller (1992)

Developed by de Shazer and associates at the Brief Family Therapy Center in Milwaukee, Wisconsin, solution-focused therapy is fundamentally different from most other types of family therapy in that it is not problem focused. Rather, it has an emphasis on solutions or what is not problematic. The development of solution-focused therapy is a continual, recursive process at the Brief Family Therapy Center (BFTC) consisting of therapy, research, theorizing, and training. There is no other common label for this model.

HISTORICAL INFLUENCES

Steve de Shazer states that the work of Milton Erickson served as the primary foundation of solution-focused therapy. Developments in this model have extended Erickson's concepts and techniques. In the mid-1970s, de Shazer worked at the Mental Research Institute and was thus influenced by the work of its researchers. In the late 1970s, a group of individuals in Milwaukee with de Shazer and Insoo Kim Berg at the nucleus started the Brief Family Therapy Center. Continuous theorizing, practice, and research at the Brief Family Therapy Center have led to refinements in solution-focused therapy practice and theory. Additional key individuals in solution-focused therapy include Eve Lipchik, Michele Weiner-Davis, Bill O'Hanlon, and Scott Miller.

PHILOSOPHY

The philosophy behind the solution-focused therapy model is based on the idea that change is constant and inevitable. A constructivist epistemology is assumed, positing that reality is co-created by the therapist and the client in the therapeutic conversation. A future orientation is primary in therapy, and there is minimal emphasis on the past except for what has previously worked. Binary logic (i.e., either/or) is replaced with systemic thinking (i.e., both/and). The emphasis in therapy is on what is possible and changeable rather than what is impossible and intractable.

According to this model, minimal steps are necessary to initiate change, and once this process is started, further changes will be generated by the client (i.e., "ripple effect" from systems theory). The systemic orientation of the model emphasizes positive feedback (i.e., change making, morphogenesis-type processes) rather than stability and homeostasis. And the notion of wholism, such that a change in one part of the system will affect other parts and relationships in the system, is emphasized. Solutions to problems are more similar than different from each other despite a diversity of presenting problems. And the emphasis in therapy is on action (i.e., doing something), not on insight or effect.

THEORETICAL TENETS

The model posits that the solutions people are using are the problem, not the presenting problems themselves. Hence, it focuses on solutions and competencies rather than problems. Proponents of the model feel that humans have the capacity within themselves to solve their own problems and that the therapist's role is to unveil or amplify nonproblematic patterns. It is not necessary that the solutions relate to the problem or to the cause of the problem.

The presenting concern that brought the family to therapy is called the complaint. The complaint is viewed behaviorally at face value; no underlying pathology is necessarily indicated by the complaint. Problems are maintained by clients' rigid adherence to doing more of what they believe will fix the problem.

Behaviors, perceptions, thoughts, and feelings that contrast with the complaint and have the potential of leading to a solution if amplified by the therapist or increased by the client (Lipchik, 1988) are referred to as exceptions. Solutions are processes that begin to develop once the problem is dissolved and what happens once the client's goal is met (de Shazer, 1988). The quicker and more effortless the solution the better. More complex means to solve problems should be used only if simpler ones have failed. If one solution doesn't work, try another.

Three types of clients are identified in solution-focused therapy. They are:

❖ *Visitors:* A classification of clients characterized by no overt complaints whose rationale for being in therapy involves someone telling them to be there. Visitors are complimented and are given no tasks.

❖ *Complainants:* A classification of clients characterized by their expectation of some solution of the problem through the process of therapy. Complainants are given observational and thinking tasks. Clients' cooperation in therapy and their desire for improvement are givens—hence, de Shazer's proclamation that client resistance is "dead" (de Shazer, 1988).

❖ *Customers:* A classification of clients characterized by their wanting to do something about the complaint. Customers are given behavioral tasks.

In solution-focused therapy, cooperation is an underlying tenet of the model. This involves a therapeutic stance in which the client is conceptualized as always working toward solutions. The therapist promotes cooperation in the relationship by using interventions that correspond with the clients' manner of cooperating. For example, if the client is a complainant, thinking or observational tasks are used to increase cooperation.

"Differences that make a difference" are actively sought by the therapist. This phrase is used to describe a class of noncomplaint conditions that may lead to solutions. The rapid resolution of complaints is probable with solution-focused therapy and will occur quickly. There are many ways to look at a situation; no one way is more correct than another. In solution-focused therapy, meanings are negotiable; the goal of therapy is to choose meanings that lead to change.

FUNCTIONAL AND DYSFUNCTIONAL EFFECTS ON FAMILIES

Solution-focused therapy is a non-normative model; therefore it does not posit what a "functional family" should look like. Even though de Shazer probably would not use the term *dysfunction,* he does note that problems in families are maintained by families doing more of what they incorrectly believe will rectify the situation. Problems can also be perpetuated through an expectation that things will recur or not change, a self-referential paradox.

ASSESSMENT AND DIAGNOSIS

Since assessment and diagnosis typically focus on problems and solution-focused therapy is not problem focused, the conventional usage of these terms is not applicable. However, de Shazer does describe a process called "disciplined observation" in which the solution-focused therapist closely watches in-session phenomena (e.g., client conceptual frame, exceptions, client status as visitor/complainant/customer, and client-therapist fit) so observed patterns can be used to promote solutions.

GOALS OF TREATMENT

Solution-focused therapy has the primary goal of addressing the family's presenting concern. Goal attainment is determined by the family's self-report of an improved state of affairs. Frequently this may be assessed on the basis of the family's subjective estimate of improvement; de Shazer and Molnar (1984) note:

> If clients perceive a change, then, in terms of their problems (for clinical and perhaps epistemological purposes), there is a change, whether or not there is an observable behavioral change. (Of course, perceptible, behavioral change is good evidence.) (p. 303)

Formation of goals with the family is a crucial component of the solution-focused model and begins in the first session. It is preferable that the goals be specific, measurable, attainable, and challenging. However, de Shazer has reported that approximately two-thirds of the families offer vague goals in the first session. Following the description of the goal, de Shazer works backwards from this target to promote behaviors compatible with this end state. For example, if a client reported that therapy would be complete when he or she increased socialization, the work in therapy could involve encouraging those types of behaviors in the present.

The process of measuring improvement toward goal attainment is more important than the desired outcome state. An accurate measure of improvement allows for clear feedback regarding the efficacy of therapeutic direction and keeps therapy from being too open-ended. Upon attainment of a satisfactory condition relevant to the family's goal (as determined in the dialogue between family and therapist), therapy is terminated.

TREATMENT PROCESS

The evolution of the treatment process in solution-focused therapy has been guided by Ockham's Razor; "What can be done with fewer means is done in vain with many." Consequently, the average number of sessions at the BFTC has decreased from six to five as the treatment process has become more efficient. A fundamental tenet of solution-focused therapy is that solutions have more in common with each other (as opposed to differences) regardless of the differences among the presenting complaints. This belief allows for the use of general treatment processes irrespective of the presenting concern. Although allowing for variation to best fit the particular needs of the family and the style of the therapist, the treatment process follows a fairly structured course. A typical first session would begin with these three tasks:

❖ *Opening:* Do introductions, structure the sessions, begin to develop fit.

❖ *Statement of complaint:* Collect specific information from each family member present about the complaints to generate later opportunities for exceptions and solutions. Have the family rank the complaints by prioritizing what should be addressed first, second, and so on.

❖ *Discussion of exceptions:* The family describes what is happening when the complaint is not present. Much detailed information regarding nonproblematic times, locations, activities, and participants will allow for greater flexibility for solution generation.

Note that throughout the first three stages the therapist uses solution language and questions that presuppose change and emphasize exceptions, solutions, and strengths.

Once the therapist has sufficient background information, the therapist will use the miracle question (asking the family how things would be different if a miracle occurred and the problem was solved) to encourage the family to think about change. Scaling questions may also be asked at this time, for example, asking the family to rate the severity of the presenting problem on a continuum from 1 (bad) to 10 (good).

After this period of information gathering, the therapist consults with a team or uses the time individually to organize ideas and develop compliments and tasks. When the therapist returns, compliments are given to the family. For example, the therapist would say to the family, "The therapy team and I want to acknowledge your work to keep the family members interacting with each other." This kind of positive reinforcement is typical of this model and sets the family up to be responsive to the homework tasks the therapist suggests. For example, a client designated as a "complainant" could be instructed to observe how things are different when the younger children receive more attention from their older sibling.

Later sessions follow a similar format except that progressively less time is devoted to discussion of the complaint and more time is spent on exceptions and solutions. A typical session would follow this pattern:

❖ *Opening:* "What is different this week compared to our last session?" Check on clues (i.e., homework tasks from the previous session).

❖ *Exceptions:* Continue to elicit, recognize, discuss, and amplify occasions in which the complaint is nonexistent or diminished. If necessary, re-examine the complaint to generate more opportunities for exceptions.

❖ *Scaling:* Accentuate any improvements over previous estimates. Process differences among family members, scaling to underscore the change. For example, "Mrs. Jones, your husband noted a change from a 2 to a 6 and you had a change from a 2 to a 3; what is he seeing that you are not seeing?"

❖ *Break*

❖ *Compliments*

❖ *Clues or homework*

The structured nature of solution-focused therapy has been refined by the creation of decision-making models and computer programs that suggest interventions in the treatment process based on therapist observations of the family. This output is called the "central map" of solution-focused therapy (de Shazer, 1988). For example, if the family is able to describe exceptions to the complaint that are predictable and controllable, the central map would indicate that the therapist should encourage "more of the same" behaviors that are associated with the exceptions.

The time parameters for a typical solution-focused therapy session are structured as follows: presession preparation, 40 minutes with the family, 10-minute consultation break, 10 minutes with the family to deliver the compliments and clues. The therapy team behind the mirror (when used) is conceptualized as being in charge of treatment, not as being merely observers or consultants.

TECHNIQUES

The team at the BFTC have developed interventions through application and research that have demonstrated clinical utility. Once a generalizable intervention is designed for a particular case and found effective, the team attempts to replicate it by using it in other appropriate situations. When a pattern of usefulness emerges, it is time to think about and study what is going on that makes the intervention useful (de Shazer & Molnar, 1984, p. 297). De Shazer notes that all interventions in solution-focused therapy are similar in that they all help clients experience change—changing behaviors, perceptions, and judgments.

Deconstructing refers to creating doubt in the client's frame of reference regarding the complaint, particularly if the frame is global, such that an expectation for change is created and new behaviors become possible. The three purposes for breaking down a global frame are that

❖ the therapist is showing his or her acceptance of the client just as he or she is by listening closely and carefully asking questions,

❖ the therapist is attempting to introduce some doubt about the global frame, and

❖ the therapist is searching for a piece of the frame's construction upon which a solution can be built. (de Shazer, 1988, p. 102)

The content of the therapeutic dialogue that deals with what is different or improved in the client's life is referred to as change talk. The therapist promotes this kind of talk to increase the client's experience of change. A directive given to the client to "do something different" (de Shazer & Molnar, 1984) is used by the therapist to encourage another response from the client's repertoire and provide a new way to attack the problem. This directive is intentionally vague so that clients will choose to do something that fits for them rather than run the risk of the therapist giving a directive outside the clients' frame.

The therapist will also advise the client to "pay attention to what you do when you overcome the temptation or urge to . . . (perform the symptom or some behavior associated with the complaint)" (de Shazer & Molnar, 1984). This technique is used when clients believe the complaint is out of their control. The intervention has a presupposition that there will be exceptions to the complaint and focuses client attention on the exceptions.

Circular questions are used in a manner similar to the Milan approach. Basically, circular questions ask one member to comment on or speculate about other family members' beliefs, feelings, and behavior. Examples of circular quesitons are:

❖ If your sister were to get married, who would miss her the most?

❖ If I ask your father, will he agree with your sister or your mother?

❖ John, what do you think has kept your mother from hearing your complaints?

(Horne & Passmore, 1991, p. 244)

When clients assume their response is the only logical thing to do and they feel stuck, the therapist may suggest that "a lot of people in your situation would have . . ." (de Shazer & Molnar, 1984, p. 302). This is frequently called *normalyzing*. By talking in this way, the therapist redefines stability as the most difficult alternative and advocates for change as being the better path toward the desired stability.

The miracle question is used to encourage thought about change, elicit solution-related information, and provide a standard by which to note changes. The miracle question is presented like this: "Suppose that one night, while you were sleeping, there was a miracle and this problem was solved. How would you know? What would be different? How will your husband know without your saying a word to him about it?" (de Shazer, 1988, p. 5).

Utilization is a key concept and class of technique derived from Milton Erickson. Conceptually, de Shazer defines it as "utilizing what the client brings with him(her) to meet his(her) needs in such a way that the client can make a satisfactory life for himself/herself" (de Shazer, 1985, p. 6). In terms of interventions, this entails using whatever the client does that is effective, good, right, or fun relevant to the goal of developing a solution. For example, if the client has a gift for organizing and classifying, this talent could be utilized in the service of solution development by having him or her categorize things that occur when the complaint does not.

Having the family provide numerical ratings regarding the state of affairs in the family (it may or may not involve the complaint) is called scaling. For example, a therapist may ask each family member, "On a scale of 1 to 10, with 1 being as bad as it could be and 10 being as good as it could be, where do you rate the situation now?" Ongoing scaling used in sessions presupposes change and provides feedback on differences among the family.

A structured component of the therapy session, the consultation break occurs approximately 40 minutes into the session. The therapist leaves the family and consults with the team (or with him- or herself if a team approach is not used) regarding the delivery of compliments and clues to the family immediately following the break. De Shazer reports that the break is similar to a trance-inducing experience for the family in that waiting for the therapist increases their receptivity to the messages delivered.

Compliments are statements delivered from the therapist to the family following the consultation break regarding what the therapist or the team sees the family doing that is good. The purpose of compliments is to build a "yes set" (de Shazer, 1982) in the client to promote the acceptance of a therapeutic task. For example, to set the stage for upcoming directives (i.e., clues), a therapist might say, "The team and I are very impressed with the degree of caring you show for your kids by your constant concern."

A formula first session task is used at the conclusion of the first therapy session. A clue or homework task typically used for families that have difficulty identifying exceptions would be presented like this: "Between now and next time we meet, we would like you to observe, so that you can describe to us next time, what happens in your family that you want to continue to have happen" (de Shazer, 1985, p. 137). Clues and homework tasks are directives delivered to clients subsequent to the compliments after the consultation break. The nature of the clue is contingent upon the classification of the clients (i.e., complainants get observation tasks, customers are given behavioral tasks, and visitors are not given tasks) and their individual characteristics that are most likely to promote solutions.

ROLE OF THE THERAPIST

The role of the therapist in solution-focused family therapy is:

- ❖ to assist the family to uncover and amplify exceptions and solutions to the presenting complaint;
- ❖ to promote an atmosphere where change is expected and belief in the family is unequivocal;
- ❖ to present self as warm, caring, active, and directive; and
- ❖ to terminate therapy as quickly as is warranted clinically.

EVALUATION OF THE SOLUTION-FOCUSED FAMILY THERAPY MODEL

Solution-focused therapy is appealing given the current zeitgeist in the health care and insurance fields because it tends to be brief, pragmatic, and cost-effective. The evaluation of in-session phenomena and therapeutic outcome that is a part of solution-focused therapy is an integral component of the recursive process of therapy, research, and theorizing. The aim of this built-in evaluation is to continue to refine solution-focused therapy such that it becomes more productive and more efficient. As previously noted, this has resulted in the average number of sessions at the BFTC decreasing from 6 to 5 (de Shazer, 1988).

An example of the process evaluation is described in de Shazer and Molnar (1984). Client response to the first session formula intervention was as follows:

> Of these, 50 (89%) clients reported something worth continuing had happened (the range was from 1 worthwhile event to 27, most frequently 5 to 7 events were reported), while 6 (11%) said nothing worth continuing had happened. (p. 300)

Outcome research performed at the Brief Family Therapy Center reported by Wylie (1990) led to the following results:

> Of 69 cases receiving 4 to 10 sessions, 64 clients, or nearly 93 percent, felt they had met or made progress on their treatment goal (about 77 percent of the 64 met the goal, and more than 14 percent made progress). At the 18-month follow-up, of all 164 clients (94 percent of whom had had 10 or fewer sessions), about 51 percent reported the presenting problem was still resolved, while about 34 percent said it was not as bad as when they had initiated therapy. In other words, about 85 percent of the clients reported full or partial success. (pp. 29–30)

This model has been applied successfully to a diversity of presenting concerns including depression, substance abuse, hallucinations, behavioral concerns with children, and marital discord (de Shazer, 1988). Criticisms of the model include the danger of clients denying or minimizing valid problems due to the therapist's emphasis on solutions, a possible inaccurate assumption that all concerns brought to therapy need to be "solved" (e.g., experiences such as loss cannot be solved but can be explored, experienced, and integrated), and questions regarding outcome claims.

REFERENCES

Berg, I. K. (1990). *A guide to practice: Constructing solutions in in-home treatment.* Milwaukee: Brief Family Therapy Center.

Berg, I. K., & Miller, S. (1992). *Working with the problem drinker: A solution-focused approach.* New York: W. W. Norton.

de Shazer, S. (1982). *Patterns of brief family therapy: An ecosystemic approach.* New York: The Guilford Press.

de Shazer, S. (1985). *Keys to solutions in brief therapy.* New York: W. W. Norton.

de Shazer, S. (1988). *Clues: Investigating solutions in brief therapy.* New York: W. W. Norton.

de Shazer, S. (1991). *Putting differences to work.* New York: W. W. Norton.

de Shazer, S., & Molnar, A. (1984). Four useful interventions in brief family therapy. *Journal of Marital and Family Therapy, 10*(3), 297–304.

Lipchik, E. (1988). Interviewing. In E. Lipchik (Ed.), *Purposeful sequences for beginning the solution-focused interview* (pp. 105–117). Rockville, MD: Aspen.

Wylie, M. S. (1990). Brief therapy on the couch. *Family Therapy Networker, 14*(2), 26–31.

Adlerian Family Therapy

❖ **MAJOR THEORISTS:** ❖
Don Dinkmeyer and Jon Carlson

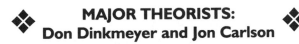

PRIMARY SOURCES FOR FURTHER READING

Fundamentals of Adlerian Psychology, Dreikurs (1953)
Raising a Responsible Child, Dinkmeyer & McKay (1973)
STEP/Teen Parents' Guide, Dinkmeyer & McKay (1982)
Adlerian Family Counseling, Christensen & Schramski (1983)
Time for a Better Marriage, Dinkmeyer & Carlson (1984)
Systems of Family Therapy: An Adlerian Integration, Sherman & Dinkmeyer (1987)
The Parents' Handbook, Dinkmeyer & McKay (1989)
"Adlerian Family Therapy," Dinkmeyer & Dinkmeyer (1991)

Initially developed by Alfred Adler and his student Rudolf Dreikurs, Adlerian family therapy is distinguished from Adlerian family counseling in that Adlerian family therapy involves the therapist seeing the entire family privately whereas Adlerian family counseling emphasizes parent education and prevention of psychopathology. Despite sharing some basic concepts, the processes of Adlerian family therapy and Adlerian family counseling are different. This chapter will focus on Adlerian family therapy.

Adler's work, originally termed *individual psychology*, served as a prototype for later models of family therapy including structural, multigenerational, and communications models. Adler acknowledges that his personal experiences when growing up influenced his theory of personality and therapy. As a child, he was sickly and had several brushes with death. Adler felt physically inferior to his younger brother and learned to compensate for these feelings through mastery in other areas. He also acknowledged the jealousy he felt toward his brother, whom he perceived as his mother's favorite. Themes of inferiority and a compensatory striving for significance in a social context pervade theory and practice in individual psychology and Adlerian family therapy.

Adlerian family therapy continues to be promoted and refined by individuals including Don Dinkmeyer, Sr., Don Dinkmeyer, Jr., Robert Sherman, and Jon Carlson. Numerous professional journals contain work relevant to Adlerian family therapy, particularly the two journals *Individual Psychology* and the *Journal of Individual Psychology.*

HISTORICAL INFLUENCES

In his professional life, Adler split with his former teacher Sigmund Freud over differences regarding fundamental human motives. Adler proceeded to develop his own theory of personality, which had a strong emphasis on family and social influences. "He called his theory Individual Psychology, referring to the essential unity of the person and of all persons within the social system" (Dinkmeyer & Dinkmeyer, 1991, p. 384).

Clinics established by Adler in Vienna around 1922 were among the first for couples and marriage therapy. Dreikurs came to Chicago in 1937 and continued to promote Adlerian family therapy in the United States. Dreikurs initiated the development of Family Education Centers, which were designed to promote counseling and education of families as well as train Adlerian practitioners. Currently, the North American Society of Adlerian Psychology and the Alfred Adler Institute of Chicago continue to promote individual psychology throughout North America.

PHILOSOPHY

The philosophy behind Adlerian family therapy posits that both individuals and social systems are holistic and indivisible in nature, that behavior is purposive and interactive, and that the individual seeks significance by belonging within a social system.

The prototypical social system is the family. Humans are inherently social and desire to help one another. The individual's personality unfolds within the context of the family and its interactions.

In the Adlerian family therapy model, perception is subjective, and individuals create meaning from their own experience. However, behavior is always comprehensible when viewed from within the logic of the family's perspective.

Problems in families result from a lack of worth or acceptance from others in the family. Therefore, treatment is an educative process that promotes growth and change. Change in family therapy is effected by addressing interactions within the family system. The interpersonal system is the focus of therapy.

THEORETICAL TENETS

The focus in Adlerian family therapy is on the social meaning of behavior and its purposiveness as expressed in the family's style of life (Horne & Passmore, 1991). All behavior has the underlying intention of overcoming feelings of inferiority and attaining superiority. This process of striving for significance originates in the individual's family of origin and is continued within the context of the family of procreation.

The patterns and themes of interaction that make up family organization and functioning are termed the family constellation. Birth order, sibling rivalry, and gender role are factors integral to the concept of family constellation. Birth order refers here to the meanings individuals and the family give to the position in the family. The specific meaning that is attributed is variable contingent upon particular family factors, yet birth order position is associated with certain general characteristics (e.g., the oldest child is typified as the achiever). Sibling rivalry is a normal process occurring in families and is due to differences among members and the individuals' personal striving for significance. Gender role refers to the expectations of how a male or female is expected to behave as modeled and mandated in the context of the multigenerational family. The individual's degree of rejection of his or her gender role can lead to confusion and conflict.

Family dynamics includes a wide variety of concepts related to the interplay of structural and functional components in the family system:

❖ *Power:* The lines of movement through which the family and each of its members strive toward goals. Mechanisms in the family through which power is channeled include decision making, manipulation, and negotiation.

❖ *Boundaries and intimacy:* The degree of physical and emotional closeness and inclusion or exclusion among family members.

❖ *Coalitions:* Two or more people joined together for mutual support or to oppose one or more other individuals. These arrangements may take the form of open alliances or hidden collusions.

❖ *Roles:* Reciprocal characteristic patterns of social behavior that members of a system expect of one another.

❖ *Rules:* Implicit or explicit guidelines that determine what behavior is acceptable or not acceptable in a family. Rules are related to family value systems and may vary with different roles in the family. Natural or logical consequences provide corrective feedback.

❖ *Complementarities and differences:* Dissimilar roles in a family may be integrated by a process of cooperative reciprocity. Individual differences among members of a system can lead to an interaction of thesis and antithesis, and ultimately result in a new synthesis.

❖ *Similarities:* Qualities of a family including shared vocabulary and a common perception of experience that enhance family cohesiveness and identity.

❖ *Myths:* A family's subjective representational model of reality. Rules and roles in a family arise from the family's myths.

❖ *Patterns of communication:* Verbal and nonverbal communications form the basis of interactions in a family. Faulty communication due to double messages, withholding information, or overgeneralizing can lead to misunderstanding and problems in the system.

FUNCTIONAL AND DYSFUNCTIONAL EFFECTS ON FAMILIES

A functional family is typified by democratic processes, where the parents are the leaders of the family yet the children have input relevant to family matters. Family rules are developed through discussion and agreement. Children can begin to participate in this process in a manner compatible with their capabilities as early as the age of 2 years. The parents establish natural and logical consequences so that the result of a child's behavior provides corrective feedback.

In a functional family, the growth and development of the family and its members are promoted. Respect for the integrity of the individual is valued as well as the family's cooperative striving for the common good. Dinkmeyer and Carlson (1993) provides this formula for a happy marriage: marital happiness equals self-esteem, plus social interest, plus a sense of humor and perspective ($MH = SE + SI + SH$).

A dysfunctional family is characterized by qualities opposite those attributed to a functional family. Specific manifestations vary with the particular family, yet general problems include:

❖ power struggles with parents who lack control or exert autocratic leadership,

❖ poor communication with blaming and little problem resolution,

❖ discouragement,

❖ lack of skills, and

❖ self-perpetuating negative feedback loops.

A dysfunctional family does not adequately meet the needs of the individual or the family as a whole. A family system that does not instill a sense of worth within a member may result in that person seeking significance through destructive, dysfunctional means.

ASSESSMENT AND DIAGNOSIS

An Adlerian family therapist is interested in acquiring information regarding the family's goals, priorities, patterns of interaction, individual and family life style, and the function the symptom serves in the system.

Strengths and resources in the family are also explored and elucidated. Typical questions the therapist will attempt to answer in the assessment phase of treatment include (Sherman & Dinkmeyer, 1987):

❖ What does each family member see as the main challenge or issue faced by the family?

❖ What does each person want to have happen in the family relationship?

❖ Identify the family atmosphere. Is the family atmosphere autocratic, democratic, permissive, friendly, or hostile?

❖ What are the life styles, games, and patterns that are revealed in the transactions between people?

Numerous methods can be employed in the assessment process. These methods are explained in the discussion of techniques.

GOALS OF TREATMENT

The overall goal of Adlerian family therapy is to promote beneficial change in individual members and in the family as a whole and to promote an ongoing process of improvement. Specific goals differ with each family; however, general goals may include these identified by Sherman and Dinkmeyer (1987):

❖ Promote new understanding and insight about purposes, goals, and behavior.

❖ Enhance skills and knowledge in areas such as communication, problem solving, and conflict resolution.

❖ Increase social interest and positive connections with others.

❖ Encourage commitment to ongoing growth and change.

Sherman and Dinkmeyer (1987) suggest that goals of Adlerian family therapy are attained by change at several levels:

❖ in perceptions, beliefs, values, and goals;

❖ in place, structure, and organization;

❖ in social interest, feelings, and participation;

❖ in skills and behavior; and

❖ in the use of power.

TREATMENT PROCESS

The treatment process can be organized into four phases (Sherman & Dinkmeyer, 1987):

1. *Joining and structuring.* The therapist gains access to the family system and sets the stage for the remainder of the therapeutic process.
2. *Assessment.* Information is gathered and tentative hypotheses about family dynamics are formulated.
3. *Developing awareness and reorientation.* The family gains increased understanding of problems and continues the change process.
4. *Commitment and termination.* Changes achieved in therapy are solidified, and the therapist begins to disengage from the family system.

TECHNIQUES

Techniques in Adlerian family therapy are adapted to the specific needs and goals of the family. Various techniques can be employed throughout the different phases of the treatment process; however, they will be noted here in association with the stage in the treatment process at which they are most commonly used.

The first phase of treatment is the joining and structuring stage. Techniques employed in this phase of treatment include:

❖ Joining and establishing rapport with the family by making contact with each family member in the system and validating his or her concerns.

❖ Using encouragement to enhance members' self-esteem by identifying strengths and assets.

❖ Reframing symptomatic behavior to offer the members a new perspective on family dynamics.

❖ Establishing the rules of therapy and the role of the therapist.

❖ Formulating tentative treatment goals.

❖ Developing a contract for the therapeutic process.

The second phase of the treatment process is assessment. Assessment techniques include:

❖ Direct observation of family behaviors in the session.

❖ Family self-report of interactions.

❖ Results of tests and inventories, e.g., Life Style Scale, Marital Inventory (Kern, 1990).

❖ Tracking, a probing technique in which the therapist asks each family member in turn to describe how a behavior pattern begins. Ultimately each person's role in creating and maintaining the pattern becomes evident.

❖ Examination of a typical day in the family. This outlines in detail daily aspects of their life and reveals much about family structure and functioning.

❖ Preparation of a genogram. This provides a visual representation of the multigenerational family history and includes information about birth order, patterns of interaction, and family themes.

❖ Early recollections. In this projective type of assessment technique family members are asked to recall their earliest recollections. The recollections produced occur within the context of current situations and, therefore, have relevance to present issues (e.g., worldview, life style, or themes).

❖ Metaphors, imagery, and fantasy. These are rich sources of indirect family information. The symptomatic behavior itself is a metaphor for the family's dynamics. Therapists can increase their understanding of family issues by attending to analogical meaning expressed in family language and behavior.

❖ Sharing tentative hypotheses with the family regarding the purpose of various family behaviors. This is done in the spirit of promoting insight and checking the accuracy of the hypotheses.

Developing awareness and reorganization constitute the third stage in the therapy process. This is typically viewed as the working-through stage of therapy. Techniques used in this stage enable the family to find more effective solutions to problems and enhances relationships such that a new family identity is initiated.

The therapist promotes improved family communication by asking all family members to adhere to these communication guidelines (Dinkmeyer & Dinkmeyer, 1991):

❖ Speak for yourself, and do not suggest what others may think or feel.

❖ Speak directly to others, not through a third party or in vague generalities.

❖ Do not scapegoat or blame.

❖ Listen and be empathic.

❖ Continue to build improved communication in the family.

Interpretations regarding family structure and functioning are outlined by the therapist. The therapist interprets findings from the assessment phase back to the family. Typically, interpretations are positively framed such that validation occurs for each family member and for the system as a whole.

At the end of the session, the therapist may provide a synopsis of what he or she learned in the session and encourage the family to do the same. This summarizing promotes family learning and provides an ongoing assessment of the family's progress in therapy.

Goal setting flows naturally out of the family's reaction to the therapist's interpretations. Each family member is responsible for his or her behavior change, and personal goals should be concrete and operational. Individuals also state what they will do for other family members and for the family as a whole. The therapist assists members in making goals realistic, attainable, and sequential.

Differences among family members are reframed as representing an increased number of possibilities and potential solutions; therefore differences are positive resources in the system. The therapist models a democratic interaction process that enables the family to identify differences and work toward agreement. Three specific techniques are taught to the family to assist them with negotiating differences:

❖ Individuals will periodically acquiesce graciously to the needs of the others. If all members practice this, each member will get what he or she wants a reasonable amount of the time.

❖ Compromise such that each member gets a bit of what he or she wants.

❖ Acknowledge that no agreement is possible and work toward agreement on a related goal.

Reorganizing places and roles in the system is a technique designed to help individuals give up dysfunctional roles and replace them with more functional roles. Some techniques used to accomplish this include: dramatizing the existing role, family sculpting, prescribing a role reversal, and renegotiating a new role.

Obstacles to attainment of therapy goals may include a lack of skills or information, fear of failure or success, longstanding family patterns, or resistance. These obstacles can be surmounted by employing the following techniques:

❖ teaching and practicing skills in the session,

❖ reframing problematic behavior with a positive connotation to change its meaning in the system,

❖ altering the modality the family uses to deal with an issue by employing games, dreams, fantasy, and role playing, or

❖ prescribing a ritual that uses a family myth in a new way.

Adlerian family therapy utilizes the following techniques to deal with resistance:

❖ *Renegotiate the goals and agreements:* Find out what the family is willing to do to change and arrange a new agreement.

❖ *Increase the family's awareness of its resistance:* Confront the family with their behavior, the consequences of their resistance, and the therapist's reaction to the resistance.

❖ *Assign a positive connotation to the resistance:* This will help avoid a power struggle; then continue with the treatment plan.

❖ *Join the resistance:* The therapist can join and even exaggerate the family's oppositional position, which will make the family switch to a cooperative position to remain resistive.

Commitment and termination represent the last phase of the treatment process. Techniques employed in this stage of treatment include:

❖ *Measurement of outcomes of therapy:* Changes in the family and movement toward the goals of therapy may be measured using observations of family interactions, self-report, and projective techniques (sculptures, dreams, and metaphor).

❖ *Refinement, reinforcement, and projection:* In the session, improvements in the family are reinforced and newly learned skills are refined. The family is encouraged to project ahead to future issues and goals and to discuss how these will be addressed.

❖ *Termination:* The therapist reiterates the family's growth in treatment and affirms their ability to successfully handle future challenges.

❖ *Follow-up:* This may take the form of a session or a telephone contact at a predetermined time following termination. The techniques used in the assessment and termination stages may be repeated in the follow-up contact (e.g., the therapist may reinforce changes and the family's competence to deal with problems), and an assessment of the family's need for further therapy can be performed.

ROLE OF THE THERAPIST

The therapist enters the family system as a partner in the change process who believes in the family's ability to grow toward improved functioning. This is conveyed by the therapist's optimistic and nonjudgmental stance toward the family. Adler's emphasis on the therapist's use of his or her entire self in an empathic manner with clients is conveyed in the following quote: "We must be able to see with his eyes and listen with his ears" (Adler, 1931, p. 72). Given the value he placed on the therapist being able to relate to the experience of being in a family, Adler thought it was beneficial but perhaps not necessary for the family therapist to have a spouse and children.

The therapist also provides structure to the therapy sessions, which conveys confidence to the family. The educational emphasis of Adlerian family therapy necessitates a therapist role that is quite active as well as being versatile and flexible. Dreikurs (1971) encourages therapists to have the "courage to be imperfect" such that they can be versatile while trusting their reactions and feelings in the family sessions.

EVALUATION

Adlerian family therapy is applicable to a diversity of presenting concerns. Strengths of the model are its comprehensiveness of scope and its flexibility of application. A positive quality unique to Adlerian family therapy is that its cousin, Adlerian family counseling, is specifically designed to have an educational and preventive focus. A relative weakness of this model, judged from a quantitative research perspective, is the paucity of nomothetic research.

This is due in part to the Adlerian tradition of being suspicious of research based on statistical methods (Mosak, 1979). Instead, Adlerians have favored a qualitative, idiographic (i.e., case method) approach to research. Case studies documenting the effectiveness of Adlerian family therapy can be found in *Individual Psychology* and the *Journal of Individual Psychology*.

The value of this model is supported indirectly by the influence individual psychology and Adlerian family therapy have had on subsequent developments in the helping professions: "Adler's concerns, ideas and methods cut across what today are called structural, strategic, communications, experimental, behavioral, cognitive, multigenerational, and ego psychology approaches to the family" (Sherman & Dinkmeyer, 1987, p. xi).

REFERENCES

Adler, A. (1931). *What life should mean to you.* Boston: Little, Brown and Company.

Ansbacher, H., & Ansbacher, R. (1956). *The individual psychology of Alfred Adler.* New York: Basic Books.

Christensen, O. C., & Schramski, T. (1983). *Adlerian family counseling: A manual for counselors, educators, and psychotherapists.* Minneapolis, MN: Educational Media Corp.

Dinkmeyer, D., & Carlson, J. (1984). *Time for a better marriage.* Circle Pines, MN: American Guidance Service.

Dinkmeyer, D., & Carlson, J. (1993). Adlerian marriage therapy. *The Family Journal, 1*(2), 144–149.

Dinkmeyer, D., & Dinkmeyer, J. (1991). Adlerian family therapy. In A. M. Horne & J. L. Passmore (Eds.), *Family counseling and therapy.* Itasca, IL: F. E. Peacock.

Dinkmeyer, D., & McKay, G. D. (1973). *Raising a responsible child.* New York: Simon & Schuster.

Dinkmeyer, D., & McKay, G. D. (1982). *STEP/teen parent's guide.* Circle Pines, MN: American Guidance Services.

Dinkmeyer, D., & McKay, G. D. (1989). *The parent's handbook* (rev. ed.). Circle Pines, MN: American Guidance Services.

Dreikurs, R. (1953). *Fundamentals of Adlerian psychology.* Chicago: Alfred Adler Institute.

Dreikurs, R. (1971). *Social equality: The challenge of today.* Chicago: Henry Regnery.

Horne, M. M., & Passmore, J. L. (1991). *Family counseling and therapy.* Itasca, IL: F. E. Peacock.

Kern, R. (1990). *Life style scale.* Coral Springs, FL: LMTI Press.

Mosak, H. H. (1979). Adlerian psychotherapy. In R. J. Corsini (Ed.), *Current psychotherapies.* Itasca, IL: F. E. Peacock.

Sherman, R., & Dinkmeyer, D. (1987). *Systems of family therapy: An Adlerian integration.* New York: Brunner/Mazel.

Integrative
Family Therapy

❖ **MAJOR THEORIST: William M. Walsh** ❖

PRIMARY SOURCES FOR FURTHER READING

Counseling Children and Adolescents, Walsh (1975)
A Primer in Family Therapy, Walsh (1980)
Childhood and Adolescence, Walsh (1984)
Family Counseling in School Settings, Walsh & Giblin (1988)
Case Studies in Family Therapy: An Integrative Approach, Walsh (1991)
The Dictionary of Family Therapy, Walsh & McGraw (1992)

Integrative family therapy (IFT) may be considered a second-generation family therapy model. Developed in 1975, IFT is one of the first blended models of family therapy. As with most theoretical models, it has changed somewhat in the past two decades. However, characteristics that were unique to the original model are still in place and differentiate it from other, more recent integrative models. No other names are used for the theory.

Educated and trained as a traditional intrapsychic therapist, William Walsh gradually shifted to systemic thinking as he incorporated into his work more of the developing ideas of the new family therapy field. His introduction to therapy was through the traditional individual models of counseling. Further professional training emphasized these individual models and gradually incorporated concepts and skills from the group therapy movement. This blending of individual and group models led to an interest and immersion in the theories of family therapy. Walsh (1980) summarizes his theoretical position by stating:

> It provides for me the most powerful methods for dealing with the human problem situations that I encounter in my professional work. However, I still rely on the concepts of individual personality development in order to understand the complexities of family living. (p. 75)

HISTORICAL INFLUENCES

IFT is an integration of several components into one consistent model, blending the ideas of several major family theorists (principally Satir, Minuchin, and Adler). Specific ideas and techniques have been selected from these models and modified to fit the philosophy and personality of this theorist. It is also an integration of these specific systems concepts with the traditional ideas of individual personality development. A practitioner of this approach may follow any one of the many intrapsychic models of therapy and combine those with the major propositions and techniques of the systemic component of IFT.

Integrative family therapy is unique in the field today in that it encourages the blending of any intrapsychic model with the four interpersonal dynamics. Most integrative theories blend only one intrapsychic model with systemic components.

PHILOSOPHY

The family is a network of specific interrelated and interdependent parts. Each person in the family, as well as groupings of individuals, is a part of the whole. The integrative family therapy model sees the family as significantly influenced by aspects of its unique heredity and environment. Each person in the family responds differently to environmental influences.

All behaviors, attitudes, values, and feelings can be either rational (enhancing) or irrational (dysfunctional) to the individual or to the family system. The context in which they are expressed is the determining factor, as aspects do not possess inherent worth in and of themselves. The total situation must be taken into consideration when an evaluation is made, including gender, race, and cultural variables.

All individuals and systems desire homeostasis. As needs arise, tension is produced in the organism. Satisfaction of those needs reduces the tension and returns the system to a more balanced state. When needs are left unsatisfied, the tension remains in the system and the organism must find other ways of returning to the balanced state. Most alternative methods attempt to reduce tension rather than satisfy needs. In integrative family therapy all behaviors of an individual or a system are seen as attempts to preserve and enhance the organism.

THEORETICAL TENETS

In IFT, family structure is a modification of the structural model developed by Salvador Minuchin (1974). The focus is on the three major subunits of the family—marital/adult, parental, and sibling —and the boundaries within and around the unit.

The marital subunit is composed of adult family members who are bonded together by emotional, sexual, or economic factors.

This subunit is the source of adult need satisfaction in the functional family. In the dysfunctional family, it is frequently the area of conflict, revenge, or avoidance.

The parental subunit is the governing body of the family, the source of decision making, goal setting, and nurturance for the entire unit. The parental subunit works best when the adults work as a team.

The sibling subunit is composed of the children of the family. Ideally, it helps produce responsible and functional adults. In a dysfunctional family, the sibling subunit can be a place of considerable suffering and acting-out behavior. Thus, it is the source of many referrals for family therapy.

Family boundaries, as described by Minuchin (1974), are an integral part of the structure of the family. Clear family boundaries allow the two-way flow of information and activity between the family and the outside world. Diffuse boundaries create over-involvement or enmeshment. Rigid boundaries provide maximum protection yet result in isolation and disengagement. Clear, diffuse, and rigid boundaries also exist within the family between the subunits.

The communication and perception (C/P) tenet of IFT is a modification of the theory of Virginia Satir (1967) and is based on Barnhill (1979). Satir emphasized communication and perception as a total process, and Barnhill discussed communication and perception as two parts of a process that he called information processing. Faulty perception is considered to be a more common dysfunction for families than is miscommunication. Communication involves sending a message. Perception has two parts: listening to the verbal or nonverbal message and understanding the implicit or explicit message. In most cases, a family will need to make changes in their communication/perception process to maximize the fulfillment of functions. By identifying the dysfunctional element, communication or perception, a more accurate treatment strategy is possible. Common communication problems are indirect, ambiguous, incomplete, or double messages. The most common perception problem is defensiveness on the part of the listener.

A role is a set of general and specific expectations that are accepted by or ascribed to each individual. A role may involve specific duties that must be performed on a regular schedule, or it may be a general way of behaving with others. Since completion of tasks is essential for a family to fulfill its various functions, appropriate expectations (role definition) and follow-through are particularly critical characteristics. If expectations are fulfilled, there are positive emotional, physical, or material consequences; when the expectations are not followed through, there are negative consequences. This sequence is called the role responsibility process (Figure 9.1).

A family theme is defined as any issue (growth producing or counterproductive) that occurs frequently for a family and that absorbs a significant amount of interest and attention of family members. All families have several identifiable major themes. Negative themes generate the initial therapeutic goals for change.

Individual personality dynamics (IPD) are the strategies that an individual uses to organize, understand, and complete the tasks of daily living. Personality dynamics are the overt and covert means used for personal need satisfaction. Functional means lead to feelings of comfort and well-being; dysfunctional dynamics distort or avoid reality in an attempt to attain immediate tension relief. The specific individual model (e.g., rational-emotive therapy, gestalt, psychodynamic, humanistic) used by the therapist fits his or her philosophy of life.

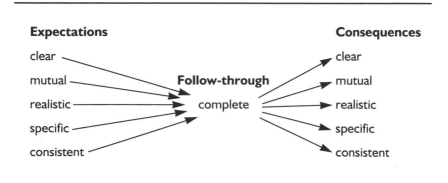

Figure 9.1   The Role Responsibility Process

FUNCTIONAL AND DYSFUNCTIONAL EFFECTS ON FAMILIES

Integrative family therapy considers several tasks that families complete to be considered well-functioning. Traditionally, the family has been the major vehicle for communicating forms of knowledge and skills. The parents and grandparents are the first teachers a child encounters. The learning process is established early, and teaching/learning continues. As children mature in healthy ways, they teach their parents new ideas and new ways of behaving. In this manner, a growth-producing teaching/learning process develops among all family members. The openness and mutuality of this process can be a barometer of a family's health.

Financial and emotional support and encouragement are equally important for the family to provide for its individual members. An absence of such support can promote insecurity and can become a source of debilitating anxiety for adults and children.

Stability is an important aspect of family functioning. Set patterns for all family members can give structure in a confusing and changeable world. Regular routines are a source of security for children. A permanent living arrangement, set times for going to bed and rising, consistent mealtimes, and seasonal traditions are all ways of providing stability in families.

Mutuality refers to the process of a family's working together for common goals. Each member knows that he or she can depend on others for help in time of need. However, each member also needs private time and space to grow as an individual, apart from the family unit. So both mutuality and privacy are important elements in the family system.

Encouraging independence is crucial for the gradual development of a healthy self-concept for each family member. Children must be taught and encouraged to function on their own in some situations, dependent only on themselves. This process should begin in early childhood with age-appropriate behaviors.

Setting unrealistic expectations for individuals or for the family unit is often a source of conflict and unhappiness. However, establishing reasonable short- and long-term goals is essential for orderly development. "Reasonable expectations" refer to those that are acceptable to all concerned; they must have a good chance of being accomplished. This is more likely to occur in a family atmosphere of open discussion and mutual decision making.

Problem solving is another important family function. The key question for this task is: "How are problems defined and resolved in the immediate present?" Does the family use a rigid process that allows little or no new input, or does the family use a flexible process that seeks out new data in an attempt to find new solutions or alternatives? Much of what happens in family therapy revolves around helping people establish and maintain rewarding problem-solving approaches to living.

The family growth process is a theoretical conceptualization that tracks healthy and unhealthy directions a family may choose. Two individuals come together, forming a relationship, usually involving a marriage commitment. Each half of the couple brings to the new relationship his or her own background from the individual's family of origin and his or her own personality dynamics. From the beginning, the relationship develops its own dynamics and characteristics; the two people develop methods for dealing with one another in the intimate relationship. They create joint ways of interacting with the outside world. Eventually, this couple may have children, broadening the number of possible interactions in the new family.

The family members' maturation and aging process produces conflict and strain. Stress is produced when, in the process of daily living, individual members interact among themselves and with the outside world. They attempt to cope with the stress and resolve conflicts on the basis of the unique relationship, the relationship's dynamics and characteristics, and new data from the outside world. All of these sources may be appropriate and functional, or they may be distorted and dysfunctional. Families with functional problem-solving abilities are less likely to be in therapy. Instead, they are able to resolve future stress and conflict on their own. Families without functional problem-solving abilities end up in dysfunction and are more likely to be in therapy.

If the family has established a functional process (i.e., appropriate relationship formation and development of unique dynamics and characteristics) and incorporates new data, it will achieve resolution by dealing with the stress and conflict. The family members are then free to continue with satisfying daily living. In IFT terminology, the successful family has a well-functioning problem-solving process. A remarriage family is particularly vulnerable at this stage. For remarriage families, both relationship formation and discovery of unique dynamics and characteristics involve complex dynamics involving more people than the traditional family. Thus, for a reconstituted family, dysfunction is more likely than achieving a successful functional process.

Dysfunction results when a family does not have a healthy problem-solving process. The immediate stress or conflict is not resolved, leaving unfinished feelings to linger. The result is interrupted daily living. Frequently, families perpetuate the dysfunction by refusing to change (rigid problem solving) or by not being knowledgeable about the alternatives available to them. Dysfunction is eventually expressed in one or more of the individuals in the family.

When the unhealthy process has occurred for years, the family may no longer be capable of containing the stress and pressure. It is at this point that a professional could enter the picture. The family may seek help on its own or another societal institution will refer the family for treatment after noticing the family's difficulties. The family may refuse to recognize the problem or seek professional help. In this instance, it is likely that the family's problems will continue or intensify. Spontaneous recovery is unlikely.

If the family chooses to seek professional help, the therapeutic intervention process begins. Ideally, a professional begins by identifying the dysfunction and then helps the family to make remediative changes. The process may be short or long term. Successful intervention results in the family members developing new ways of relating to one another, new problem-solving methods, and a greater understanding of themselves and others. After termination of therapy, the family can meet and resolve future stress and conflict.

ASSESSMENT AND DIAGNOSIS

Observation and assessment occur during the second stage of IFT, after the therapist has structured the session and made contact with each member of the family. Assessment takes place during the first two sessions.

The five characteristics of families—family structure, communication and perception, role responsibility, family themes, and individual personal dynamics—are used to develop a diagnostic picture of the family. The family unit and each individual within the unit are evaluated with regard to specific and general dynamics. The therapist identifies and isolates the specific problems that brought the family into therapy and translates them into short-term goals for the immediate future. Long-term goals arise from the pervasive, general dysfunction that causes the family pain.

The therapist's evaluation of the family is shared with them, typically during the third session, and is often in written form. The written assessment card is developed based on the theoretical tenets that then become suggested goals of treatment. The assessment card is given to each family member, and the family members give their reactions to the goals listed. Mutual goals are set, and the intervention process begins.

GOALS OF TREATMENT

The goals of treatment in integrative family therapy are to remediate specific immediate difficulties and concerns of individuals and the family unit, and to build a satisfying problem-solving process that individual members and the family unit can use to deal with future problems.

TREATMENT PROCESS

IFT is a well-defined and structured process with a mean duration of ten sessions per family. It has specific developmental stages, and each stage has certain tasks to accomplish. With an organized theoretical process, the therapist has the capacity to impose order, establish goals, and chart future directions.

The primary task of the first therapy session is structuring. The therapist asserts control from the beginning of the first encounter.

The relationship is consultative, with the therapist seen as a professional with skills who is employed by the family to assist the members in finding solutions to their individual and joint problems. By exerting initial control, the therapist instills confidence and optimism in family members regarding the potential for change to occur. Four tasks should be accomplished during the first session for the therapist to establish control yet promote an accepting, cooperative atmosphere:

❖ The therapist should be firm about the overt parameters of the contractual relationship with the family. Time and length of sessions are discussed. All family members should be encouraged to attend so the therapist can observe how they interact, introduce the entire family to the counseling process, and gather information from all family members.

❖ The therapist makes contact with each individual member and elicits help and information from him or her. Trust, acceptance, confidentiality, and unconditional positive regard are communicated to each member to build rapport.

❖ The therapist models healthy communication/perception processes. He or she is clear and specific in interactions and insists that family members behave this way also.

❖ The therapist teaches and demonstrates the basics of systems thinking to begin the transition from linear thought processes to systemic. This shift from linear to systemic thinking on the part of the family is seen as critical since the absence of systemic conceptualization may be the major reason for premature termination.

Observation and assessment constitute the next stage of the treatment process. This stage provides a diagnostic picture of family members and the unit as a whole. The various facets of this process are discussed more fully in the assessment and diagnosis section.

The intervention process is based on the assessment stage. The major intervention strategies are described in the techniques section. Some important aspects of the intervention stage include:

❖ The establishment of short-term and long-range goals that determine present and future interventions. These are shared with the family in written form on the assessment card and are discussed by all family members. The family and the therapist then accept or modify the assessment card. New data are incorporated as therapy progresses.

❖ The presentation and discussion of the assessment card. This is the beginning of the intervention stage. Each goal on the card is discussed with the family and examples from previous sessions are used to illustrate each point.

❖ The employment of therapeutic techniques. These are used to move the family through the change process as they address the goals on the assessment card.

The primary task of change maintenance is to reinforce new behaviors and patterns of interaction. The therapist may continue to use his or her intervention strategies, but these may be less active and less directive. The family begins taking more responsibility for members' present and future behavior. Time is increased between sessions as the therapist removes himself or herself from a central position in the family. The therapist assists the family in generalizing its new behaviors and insights.

Termination is indicated when a family is displaying the following behaviors: Present-day conflicts are resolved in mutually satisfying ways; members express optimism about future plans; the family sets realistic goals for the unit and for each individual member; and each member has internalized the new behaviors, attitudes, and feelings. Four-week intervals between sessions during this last stage are the norm. The following tasks are included in the termination process:

❖ The therapist reviews the family's entire therapy process and specifically reinforces the new behaviors and interactional patterns.

❖ The therapist checks each individual's feelings and attitudes toward the changes that have occurred to see that each member has personalized and internalized the changes.

❖ Future goals of the unit and of each member are discussed.

❖ The therapist presents written and verbal feedback to the family concerning his or her perception of its therapeutic process.

TECHNIQUES

Any well-accepted technique from any of the major models of family therapy may be used with the family. A sound therapeutic rationale for using a given technique is the guiding principle for the selection of any therapeutic maneuver. The technique must fit the needs and goals of the family to be genuine and productive. The following are examples of common intervention strategies:

❖ The presentation and discussion of the assessment card is the beginning of the intervention stage. Each goal on the card is discussed with the family, and examples from previous sessions are used to illustrate each point.

❖ Discussion and enactment of specific problem situations. Through discussion of recent examples of conflict situations the therapist can assist the family in generating alternative solutions for resolution. A therapist may nondirectively guide or actively manipulate a situation dependent upon the family's capacities and upon the theoretical orientation of the therapist.

❖ Use of confrontation techniques to help people communicate more accurately and effectively with one another. The therapist encourages all family members to openly and directly discuss their perceptions and reactions to situations. An atmosphere of trust and honesty develops, reducing the threat of reprisal or retribution.

❖ Use of communication checks to ensure accurate perception on the part of all family members. The therapist establishes a pattern of continually checking his or her perceptions of what has been communicated and encourages the family members to do the same. Assumptions and inaccurate perceptions should be immediately identified and corrected.

❖ Working out definite roles and expectations for each member. The therapist encourages all family members to identify both specific expectations they have for one another and specific tasks that are part of each other's roles. Negotiation may be necessary to achieve mutually satisfying positions. Consequences may need to be established for the noncompletion of tasks.

❖ Setting general or specific rules that will govern the family members' daily lives. Family members decide how they want to organize their daily living patterns.

❖ Encouraging the family to hold regular family meetings to supplement the therapeutic contracts. Initially, meetings can be used to practice and reinforce new behaviors learned in therapy. Meetings can eventually take the place of therapy.

ROLE OF THE THERAPIST

The therapist is a professional with specific skills who is employed as a consultant in assisting families regarding certain problem situations. The relationship is never power-related or adversarial. In a sense, it is a business-like arrangement that happens to involve intensely personal ideas, feelings, and behaviors.

The therapist controls the therapy session by structuring and instilling confidence and optimism in the family members regarding the potential for change to occur. The family experiences order and stability within the session.

The therapist's behavior provides role models for individuals to emulate in the session and in their outside contacts. For example, by modeling healthy communication/perception processes, the therapist teaches the family how to engage in clear and specific interactions. The therapist observes and assesses the family unit and its members to provide feedback to the family and to actively intervene in family patterns.

EVALUATION OF THE INTEGRATIVE FAMILY THERAPY MODEL

The validity and efficiency of the integrative family therapy model have been tested primarily on the basis of the experiences of the therapists and the reports of change by the families over a 20-year period. In the past ten years, a rating scale comparing the goals on the assessment card and the final evaluation of the therapist and family has been used to assess the degree of change on major family variables (Walsh, 1991). The five-point scale (1 = no goals attained, to 5 = all goals attained) is completed by the therapist after the final session. Ratings of families seen in the past decade range from 2 to 5 with a mean rating of 4.2.

A study by Walsh and Wood (1983) compared the Dynamics of Family Life Scale, an instrument based on the integrative model, to several other family measurement scales. Twenty-six families who were in family treatment because of difficulty with an adolescent member were the subjects of the study. Using statistical tests of significance, the instrument was found to be useful in identifying the degree of dysfunction in a family unit. The findings were also consistent with the independent assessments of the therapists. A high degree of consistency was observed between the variables identified in this study and in two major studies of similar instruments (Lewis, Beavers, Gossett, & Austin, 1976; Faunce & Riskin, 1970). The following correspondences were found:

❖ Functional families typically had a warm and expressive feeling tone, and they were generally more openly expressive and empathic.

❖ Low levels of conflict characterized healthier families.

❖ Clear parental coalitions were prevalent in healthy families, and subsystem composition in general was highly related to degree of dysfunction.

❖ Healthier families tended to be clear in their expressions of feelings and thoughts.

❖ The relationship between distorted perception and dysfunction was found to be stronger than the relationship between distorted communication and dysfunction.

REFERENCES

Barnhill, L. R. (1979). Healthy family systems. *Family Coordinator, 28,* 94–100.

Faunce, E., & Riskin, J. (1970). Family interaction scales. *Archives of General Psychiatry, 22,* 504–537.

Lewis, J., Beavers, R., Gossett, J., & Austin, V. (1976). *No single thread.* New York: Brunner/Mazel.

Minuchin, S. (1974). *Families and family therapy.* Cambridge, MA: Harvard University Press.

Satir, V. (1967). *Conjoint family therapy: A guide to theory and technique* (rev. ed.). Palo Alto, CA: Science and Behavior Books.

Walsh, W. M. (1975). *Counseling children and adolescents.* Berkeley, CA: McCutchan.

Walsh, W. M. (1980). *A primer in family therapy.* Springfield, IL: Charles C. Thomas.

Walsh, W. M. (1984). *Childhood and adolescence.* Berkeley, CA: McCutchan.

Walsh, W. M. (1991). *Case studies in family therapy.* Needham Heights, MA: Allyn & Bacon.

Walsh, W. M., & Giblin, N. (1988). *Family counseling in school settings.* Springfield, IL: Charles C Thomas.

Walsh, W. M., & McGraw, J. (1992). *The dictionary of family therapy.* Greeley, CO: University of Northern Colorado.

Walsh, W. M., & Wood, J. I. (1983). Family assessment: Bridging the gap between theory, research, and practice. *American Mental Health Counselors Journal, 5,* 111–120.

Descriptive Summary of Seven Additional Approaches

 **MAJOR THEORISTS:**

James Framo

Carl Whitaker

John Weakland, Paul Watzlawick, Richard Fisch,
Arthur Bodin, and Carlos Sluzki

Ivan Boszormenyi-Nagy

Samual Slipp, Jill Savage Scharff, and David Scharff

Michael White and David Epston

Harry Goolishian and Harlene Anderson

INTERGENERATIONAL FAMILY THERAPY

James Framo

Having roots in psychoanalytic thought, intergenerational family therapy explores the impact the family of origin has on the marital relationship. Similar to Bowenian family therapy, Framo's work is oriented toward increasing insight and understanding of family dynamics as they relate to unresolved issues passed down from previous generations. This model fits well with couples work, and Framo has used a group model to work with numerous couples simultaneously. Part of the effectiveness of the group approach lies in the vicarious learning that occurs as individuals observe other group members address relational concerns similar to their own.

SYMBOLIC-EXPERIENTIAL FAMILY THERAPY

Carl Whitaker

Whitaker's experience using play therapy in his work with children influenced the development of his model of family therapy. He also cites the impact of Melanie Klein (psychoanalysis with children), Gregory Bateson, Alan Watts, and Carl Jung on his work. Whitaker's approach tends to be atheoretical, pragmatic, and technically eclectic with a focus on change through a diversity of interventions. Whitaker is famous for creative and unconventional techniques used to challenge or confuse the family. Areas of emphasis in this approach include: the experience and expression of emotion in the here and now, promoting the natural growth tendency in families, and recognizing the struggle between autonomy and interpersonal belonging within the family group.

MRI STRATEGIC FAMILY THERAPY

John Weakland, Paul Watzlawick, Richard Fisch, Arthur Bodin, and Carlos Sluzki

This family therapy approach originates from the work of a diversity of pioneers in family therapy (Bateson, Satir, Haley, Jackson, and Weakland) at the MRI in Palo Alto, California. MRI strategic family therapy and de Shazer's solution-focused model are based on a common philosophical foundation. MRI strategic family therapy is strongly systemic in theory and application. The focus in this model is on effective family functioning and adaptability through periods of stress and change.

CONTEXTUAL FAMILY THERAPY

Ivan Boszormenyi-Nagy

This model strives toward integration of a systemic approach with intrapsychic approaches. The relational context of family functioning extending to many prior generations is evidenced by some of the key terms in this model: rejunctive (behaviors that promote trustworthy relatedness), disjunctive (behaviors that decrease relatedness), legacy (influences passed down from prior generations), and divided loyalty (a pathological alliance of a child with one parent against the other). While emphasis is placed on the importance of relatedness within a family system (with healthy families being fair, flexible, and equitable), the striving of the individual for autonomy within the system is recognized as well.

OBJECT RELATIONS FAMILY THERAPY

Samual Slipp, Jill Savage Scharff, and David Scharff

Based on Freudian thought and the work of later theorists (e.g., Kohut, Mahler, Fairbairn, Winnicott), object relations family therapy conceptualizes current relationship difficulties as originating in early child-parent interactions. This model attempts to bridge intrapsychic and interpersonal approaches, utilizing object relations concepts (e.g., individual development, projection, ego identity) within a relations context. The general goal of this model is to provide a therapeutic environment in which the family can understand and resolve unconscious issues that are problematic to current family functioning.

NARRATIVE THERAPY

Michael White and David Epston

This model of family therapy, based on constructivism, examines how individuals can "reauthor" their life story in a way that externalizes the concern that brought them to therapy. Therapists assist families to create new stories by asking them to explain "unique outcomes" (i.e., situations in which the "problem" is nonexistent). The process of developing new stories creates a sense of personal urgency for family members that enables them to better manage future struggles. This therapeutic process also promotes an appreciation of the subjective, "storied" nature of human existence for the family.

CONSTRUCTIVIST FAMILY THERAPY

Harry Goolishian and Harlene Anderson

Similar to narrative, this model of family therapy is based on constructivism and focuses on how individuals create their experience. Constructivist family therapy reverses the typically held position that the family system causes the problem by positing that the problem promotes the formation of a meaning system (i.e., the family system) around it. Even though a coherent model of therapy has not been explicated by the proponents of constructivist family therapy, the process of therapy conceptualizes the therapist as "participant narrative artist" involved with the family in the cocreation of new meanings.

ADDITIONAL RESOURCES

INTERGENERATIONAL FAMILY THERAPY

Framo, J. L. (1982). *Explorations in family and marital therapy: Selected papers of James L. Framo.* New York: Springer Publishing Co.

SYMBOLIC-EXPERIENTIAL FAMILY THERAPY

Whitaker, C. A., & Keith, D. V. (1981). Symbolic-experiential family therapy. In A. S. Gurman & D. P. Kniskern (Eds.), *Handbook of family therapy* (pp. 187–225). New York: Brunner/Mazel.

Whitaker, C. A., & Bumberry, W. M. (1988). *Dancing with the family: A symbolic-experiential approach.* New York: Brunner/Mazel.

MRI STRATEGIC FAMILY THERAPY

Fisch, R., Weakland, J. H., & Segal, L. (1982). *The tactics of change: Doing therapy briefly.* San Francisco: Jossey-Bass.

CONTEXTUAL FAMILY THERAPY

Boszormenyi-Nagy, I. (1987). *Foundations of contextual therapy: Collected papers of Ivan Boszormenyi-Nagy.* New York: Brunner/Mazel.

OBJECT RELATIONS FAMILY THERAPY

Scharff, D. E., & Scharff, J. S. (1987). *Object relations family therapy.* Northvale, N. J.: Jason Aronson.

Slipp, S. (1988). *The technique and practice of object relations family therapy.* Northvale, NJ: Jason Aronson.

NARRATIVE THERAPY

White, M., & Epston, D. (1990). *Narrative means to therapeutic ends.* New York: W. W. Norton.

White, M. (1993). The histories of the present. In S. Gilligan (Ed.), *Therapeutic conversations.* New York: W. W. Norton.

CONSTRUCTIVIST FAMILY THERAPY

Goolishian, H., & Winderman, L. (1988). Constructivism, autopoiesis and problem-determined systems. *The Irish Journal of Psychology, 9,* 130–143.

Anderson, H. (1993). On a roller coaster: A collaborative language systems approach to therapy. In S. Friedman (Ed.), *The new language of change.* New York: Guilford Press.

Anderson, H., & Goolishian, H. (1988). Human systems as linguistic systems: Preliminary and evolving ideas about the implications for clinical theory. *Family Process, 27,* 371–393.

INDEX